THE TOYS OF ASTRA-PHAROS

David J Booth

Copyright © David J Booth

A CIP record of this book is available from the British Library.

All Rights Reserved. No part of this work may be reproduced or utilised in any form or by any means, electronic or mechanical, including photocopying, recording or by any information storage and retrieval system, without the prior written permission of the publisher.

ISBN 978 0 9556361 0 3

Publishers Note: While every effort has been made to ensure that the information given in this book is correct the publisher does not accept responsibility for any inaccuracy. The publisher would welcome correspondence with any person having further information about the company Astra-Pharos or its products.

Published by D J Booth 2007
The Cottage,
Green Lane,
Cotton Edmunds,
Chester CH3 7QB

Printed by The Print Centre, Saltney Chester
on environmentally friendly paper.

Acknowledgements

I would like to thank: Peter Rumsey for supplying the nucleus of the literature and models in my collection; my good friend Tony Homden for much useful information and photographs of models from his extensive collection; Michael Hewitt for his recollections of the Astra-Pharos works when his father was foreman; my daughter Melanie who typed the manuscript and finally my wife Judy for her support during this project.

Preface

I was introduced to the toys of Astra-Pharos as a young boy in the early 1950s when I was given a "new anti tank gun". I was very impressed with it at the time since it outperformed all the other toy guns that I owned. It was to be almost 40 years before I saw another Astra model, when attending a toy fair in Leeds. This fort gun rekindled my enthusiasm for the toys and then I discovered that a friend at work had a small collection. He gave me a photocopy of his 1940 Astra catalogue which prompted me to start collecting the toys and to find out more about the company.

All of the early toys made prior to the military range are very difficult to find, with the 2-inch searchlight, the roundbased searchlight and the 3 light traffic signal being the most common. For the military range and the post war range I have attempted to give a rather crude guide to rarity. At the end of each model description I have graded the model with a letter in the range A to E; A being the most common and E being the most rare.

Photographs of models with an asterisk are from the collection of Tony Homden. All other photographs are of models from the author's collection.

Historical Survey

After the First World War, ex RFC pilot Frank Weldon teamed up with Charles Freeman to form two electrical engineering companies. Motolite Dynamos Ltd of Landor Road, Askew Street, London W12 and Astra Dynamo Co. Ltd of 124, Victoria Street, London SW1, where they were both directors. Astra Dynamo Co. Ltd produced a range of lighting sets and dynamos for motorcycles.

In December 1922 the trademark Pharos (number 429,005) was registered to Motolite Dynamos Ltd and eighteen months later in May 1924 the trademark ASTRA (Number 448,286) was registered to Charles Teverill Freeman and Frank Yonge Urquhart Weldon. The Pharos trademark was transferred to Astra Dynamo Co. Ltd in August 1927 and in 1929 the company together with Motolite dynamos went into voluntary liquidation. At the same time the two trademarks were transferred to Charles Freeman.

Later that year Freeman and Weldon formed a new company Astra-Pharos Ltd, trading from the old premises of Motolite Dynamos at Landor Road, Askew Street, London W12. The Landor Road site was a large end terraced house and the adjoining mid terraced property. Both had been converted into a small factory. Astra-Pharos were to remain there until the company closed down in 1975. The building was still being used as an engineering works in the mid 1990s, but by 2004 it had been refurbished and converted into flats.

The principal business of Astra-Pharos in the very early 1930s was the manufacture and sale of spotlights, "Magniflect" searchlights, side car lights, tail lights, dynamos and electric horns for motorcycles. They produced a catalogue describing and illustrating the items they sold and advertised in "The Motor Cycle".

In 1926 Bill Hewitt left school and joined Motolite Dynamos Ltd. The photograph shows him (left) standing in front of the gates to Motolite Dynamos on his first day. He stayed on during the restructuring of the company in 1929 and remained with Astra-Pharos Ltd during its entire period of toy production, finally leaving to join Vickers Ltd in 1955. By this time he had become works foreman and played a major part in developing prototypes for new toys. His son Michael remembers him bringing models home and working on them until late into the night. Sometimes when a simple model was discontinued Bill would bring examples of it, or the actual mould, home for his children to play with. Michael remembers casting small lead lighthouses and Astra model ships from the original production moulds.

William Hewitt

Toy production began in a small way in the early 1930s and at first the company did not advertise to the public, but relied on established toyshops to do it for them. The first advertisements appeared in Meccano Magazine in May 1933, Gamages selling searchlights at 3/9d and 3-light traffic signals at 3/6d. The same month Hamleys advertised the same Astra searchlight for 5/6d. By October Hamleys were also advertising a 2-light railway signal.

As Freeman and Weldon were electrical engineers, they capitalised on the public's fascination with electricity in the early 1930's and all of their early toys lit up in some way using a battery and bulb. By Christmas 1934 they had a 9-model range, which was expanding rapidly. Percy Goodwin, then trading from 27, Paper Street, London EC1, had been appointed as sole distributor for a few of the models. He must have been quite successful, because during 1935 Astra Pharos decided to increase trade by advertising under their own name and appointed Percy Goodwin, who had now moved to 80, Wood Street, London EC2, as sole distributor for all of their range. Goodwins first advertisements appeared in Meccano Magazine in November and December 1935 illustrating the range of "Astra" toys.

Over the next 12 months the company's success at toy making continued, and by December 1936 the range had expanded to 20 different models. Distribution was also improving and in his advertisement in Meccano Magazine in December 1936 Percy Goodwin listed 12 major department stores in Southern England as stockists together with all branches of Lewis's. An illustrated list of Astra toys was also available free from the Distributor.

At some time during early 1937 Astra-Pharos and Percy Goodwin Ltd parted company and Astra took over advertising and distribution of toys themselves. 1937 also saw Astra-Pharos making a brave move and abandoning most of their previous range of toys in favour of a new range of military style toys. In May of that year Charles Freeman applied for a patent to protect his invention of a breech loading, cap firing toy gun. Over the next few years, this invention was successfully used in a variety of toy guns.

PATENT SPECIFICATION

Application Date: May 4, 1937.   No. 12666/37.

Complete Specification Left: May 4, 1938.

Complete Specification Accepted: Sept. 30, 1938.

492,977

PROVISIONAL SPECIFICATION

Improved Cartridge for Firing Projectiles from Toy Firearms of all sizes

A new catalogue was introduced during the year and this assigned a number to each of the models illustrated. This numerical system was to remain unchanged for as long as toy production continued. The catalogue announced proudly "Working models as supplied to H.M. Forces for training purposes."

The first advertisement promoting the new range of toys appeared in Meccano Magazine of October 1937 and was taken out by Astra-Pharos Ltd and not Percy Goodwin. The advertisement also introduced the new logo, which was the word ASTRA mounted within a diamond shaped frame.

At this time there were obviously still stocks of the old range of toys as these were still referred to in small print in the Astra advertisements. Then in November and December 1937 Kliptico Ltd., promoting themselves as "Paramount Electrical Toys" took out whole page advertisements in Meccano Magazine illustrating the old range of Astra toys for sale.

Sales of the new range must have been encouraging because a new catalogue was bought out for 1938, which illustrated an increased range. Innovation continued in 1939 and 1940 with new models being introduced each year and less successful models being discontinued. The 1940 catalogue was the last to be produced until after the Second World War. It was overprinted later in the year with "Purchase Tax - retail prices should be advanced approx. 20%" and stickers were added listing the models which were temporarily suspended owing to the difficulty of obtaining raw materials. Finally in the Meccano Magazine of April 1942 Astra-Pharos announced that production of toys was suspended for war work. It did not resume toy making again until November 1945 when it announced that models were available in limited numbers. During the intervening period the company made parts for Vickers machine guns.

> Owing to the difficulty of obtaining raw materials, the manufacture of Models Nos. 9, 12, 23, 13, 10 and 16 has been temporarily suspended. These models should therefore not be ordered until further notice.

Advertising did not stop during the period 1942-1945, to keep their products in customers' minds; the company took out regular small display advertisements containing the ASTRA logo and the words "manufacture suspended until after the war".

As soon as toy production resumed, innovation in toy design continued. Alan Gordon Morris, one of the new directors (Charles Freeman had resigned as director some years before) applied for a patent in February 1946 to protect his invention of the automatic repeating pom pom gun.

In March 1948 Frank Weldon applied for a patent to protect his "improvements relating to toy colour light signals".

In the immediate post war years the Government of the day directed that industrial output should be exported wherever possible, to limit "home sales" and encourage exports, they increased purchase tax on toys to 100% in 1947. This meant that there was only a small supply of Astra toys available to the British market. The company in its advertising continued to apologise for the shortages right up until the end of 1951.

ASTRA
WORKING MODELS

★

Once again these splendid toys are in very short supply.

However, all good toyshops stock our models, and we suggest you pay a visit to your local Astra dealer. He may still be able to supply you with the models you require, but don't delay, as stocks are running low.

★

Sole Patentees and Manufacturers:

ASTRA PHAROS LTD.
239, Earl's Court Road, London S.W.5

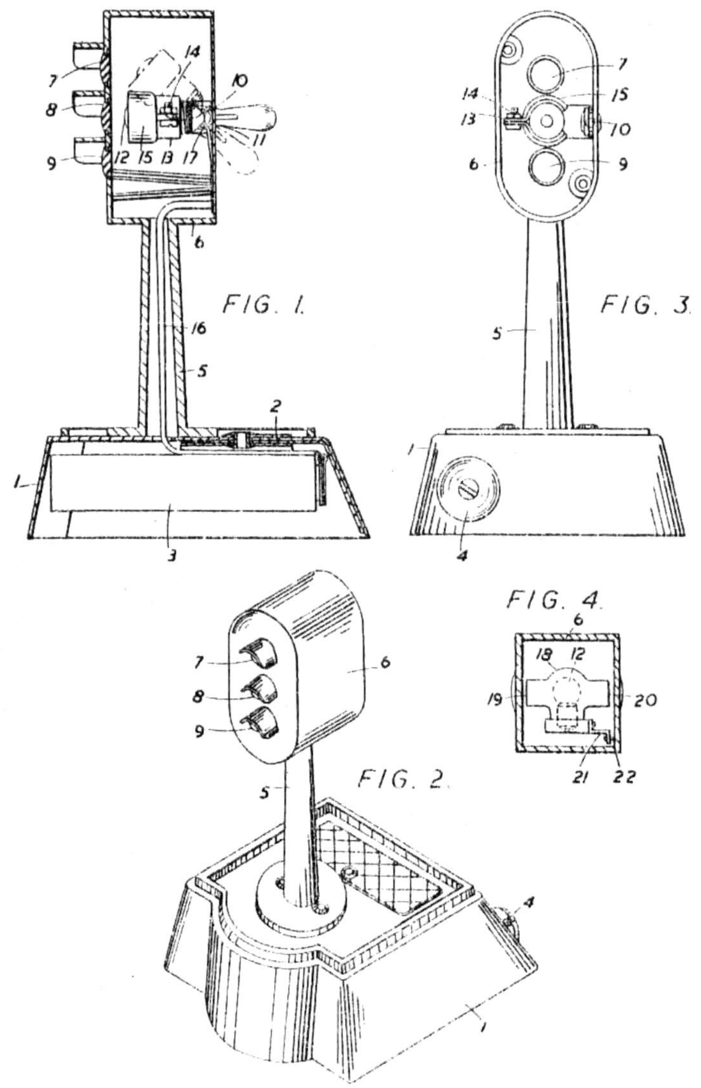
FIG. 1.
FIG. 2.
FIG. 3.
FIG. 4.
1
2
3
4
5
6
7
8
9
10
11
12
13
14
15
16
17
18
19
20
21
22

H.M.S.O. (M.F.P.)

The 1949 catalogue, printed in red, green and black ink on cream paper, was a larger more elaborate production than pre war ones. Of the 11 models described, only 5 were carried over from the pre war listing. Early 1950 saw the production of a simple leaflet printed in black, green and red ink on white glossy paper, advertising the 4 new "coloured light signals", which incorporate Frank Weldon's new patent. The leaflet also promoted the larger catalogue of "anti aircraft guns, pom pom guns and rocket guns".

At times during the early 1950's the company advertised from additional premises at 239, Earl's Court Road, London SW5. Nothing is known about this site, but it could have been a retail shop.

Over the next couple of years the pre war models were discontinued. Two new models were introduced during 1952 however, this only gave a range of 9 models. In the 1930's Astra-Pharos were an electrical engineering company that also made toys. By the end of the Second World War they were almost exclusively mechanical engineers and during the early 1950's, toy production became an ever smaller part of the business. They made a diverse selection of products ranging from props for film companies to the components of "clocking on" machines. Their last toy advertisement appeared in Meccano Magazine in January 1954 and toy production had ceased by the end of that year. Frank Weldon stayed on as director until retiring in 1962 being replaced by Dennis and Dora Wells.

Astra-Pharos Ltd ceased to trade in January 1975.

Some of the moulds for making Astra toys were sold in the 1950's, to Wend-al Toys Ltd and Johillco who both produced an inferior range of military toys from them.

The Early Years

1933

This year saw the first advertisements for toys manufactured by Astra Pharos. The well-made 2 inch diameter searchlight mounted on a 3x4 inch base was painted mid grey, with the battery being mounted underneath the base. The Astra name was mounted on a plate at the front of the base. The three light traffic signal was cast with a hollow supporting pole to take the battery. The whole model was painted black and the switching mechanism was incorporated on to the card blanking plate behind the lights.

This card was impressed with the words "Astra British Made". There are two versions of this traffic signal, one made of cast iron, the other made of cast light alloy. The two light railway signal was also painted black, but the switching mechanism and battery holder were separated and connected to the base terminals of the signal with wire.

Later in the year the familiar round based searchlight was introduced. This model in modified form was to remain in production until the 1950's. These early models were painted mid grey.

BRITISH
ASTRA
MADE
EXTRA LIFE R6 SIZE 1.5 V
Made in Britain
EXTRA LIFE R6 SIZE 1.5 V
Made in Britain
*
*

1934

This year saw the introduction of five new models. A two light traffic signal, operating on the same principle as the three light model and a more complex four way traffic signal. This black signal still supported the battery inside the pole, but the switching mechanism was mounted on top of the light. By rotating the round top the red, amber, green sequence changed on all 4 sides of the light simultaneously. Cast in to this top were the words "PAT. APP. FOR", and a metal label bearing the words "Astra British Made" was pinned across the centre.

The Morse signalling set involved the clever use of the 2 inch searchlight mounted on a new larger base fitted with a Morse key. These models were painted grey and sold in pairs with detachable tripod legs. A printed label "Astra London Made" was attached to the front of the base. The aerodrome floodlight consisted of small lamp mounted on a small conical base with a total height of 2½ inches. This grey model was very expensive at 4/6d, but came complete with a separate switch and a separate holder for two AA batteries (identical to that supplied with the railway signal). A newly designed red "Astra" roundel was fixed part way up the conical base.

The final new model for the year was a magnificent five-inch diameter searchlight mounted on a square base, which housed the battery. The model was painted grey initially, but later versions have been seen in khaki and had a wheel mounted at the front of the base, which acted as an on/off switch. A label "Astra London Made" was attached to the flat surface above the front wheel on/off switch.

13

14

15

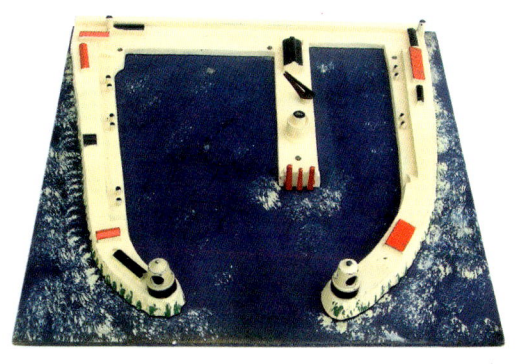

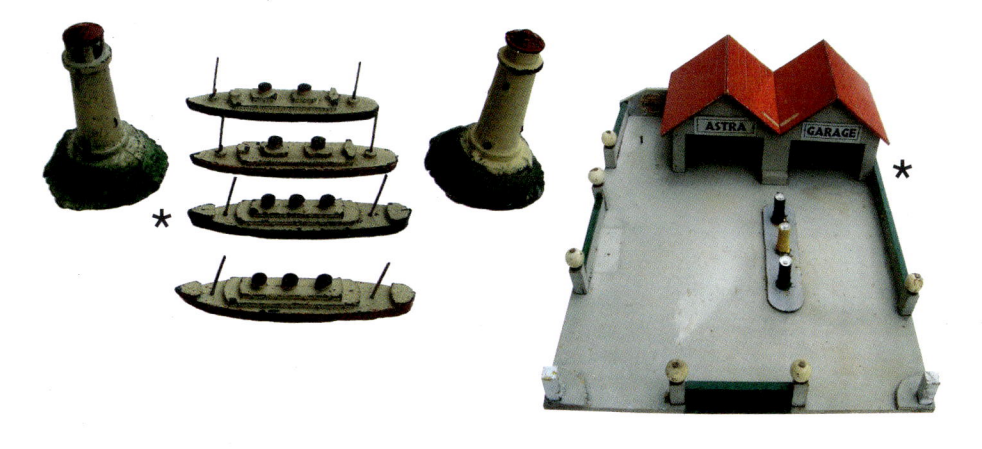

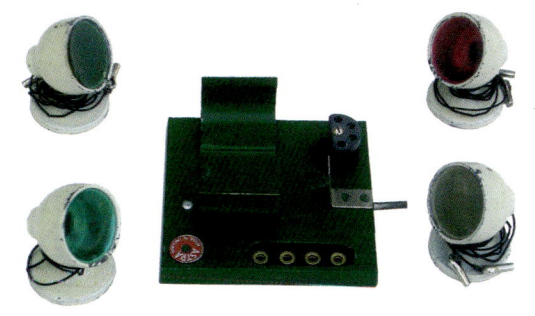

1935

This year saw the introduction of seven new models, some of which were far more complex than those produced so far. The 4 way traffic signal was discontinued and the prices of the other 2 signals were reduced from 3/9d to 2/11d and from 4/9d to 3/9d. The aerodrome floodlight was also reduced in price to a much more reasonable 1/6d , but did not include the switch and battery holder. A new 6 light traffic signal was produced to replace the discontinued model. This was operated in a similar way to the 3 light signal described previously.

A casting of a model harbour for waterline ships was produced and mounted on a 12x12-inch board, which was painted green and white to resemble the sea. With a battery connected externally, the lighthouses on either side of the harbour entrance would light up.

The "pierhead and bandstand" was also mounted on a 12x12 inch board, but this time the sea was painted blue and white and sand was glued on to make a realistic beach. An internally mounted battery allowed the pavilion and bandstand to light up. With increasing numbers of cars on the roads at this time Astra-Pharos began what was to become a range of garages. The first was a petrol filling station mounted on a 12½ x 4 ½ inch plywood board. This simple model had oil bins, compressed air plant and petrol pumps which lit up when connected to an external battery, The "Garage for Miniature Motor Cars" was mounted on a 12x10 inch plywood board and comprised a workshop with "Astra Garage" over the door and oil bins, compressed air plant and 2 petrol pumps on the forecourt. The petrol pumps lit up when connected to an external battery.

On a much larger scale was a model of a petrol pump standing 6 inches high and painted red. The battery was housed in the body of the pump and the globe at the top lit up. The final new model produced during the year was a lighthouse standing 6½ inches high mounted on an imitation rock base. Again the battery was housed in the body of the lighthouse and the light at the top switched on and off by means of a small rotating handle on the rocky base. An Astra roundel was mounted between the handle and the lighthouse.

1936

The whole of the 1935 model range was carried over into 1936. The harbour underwent two changes. At first the original casting was increased in size and detail, adding railway lines at the rear and a crane on the centre jetty. Although the 12x12-inch board was retained, it was now painted blue and white. This modification was short lived and before the year was out a completely new harbour casting was introduced, with the battery mounted within a rocky headland.

The board size of this model was increased to 14x12 inches. Two additional blue and white painted plain boards were included in the set to increase the area of the "sea". These changes required a price increase from 4/11d to 5/11d.

A new set of 4 waterline ships and two small 2 inch high lighthouses were introduced for use with the model harbour; usually these were cast in lead. An additional lighthouse in the same scale was available separately. This had a tiny bulb mounted in the top, and would light up using a remote battery.

The larger petrol pump was recast into a more modern design, but the price remained the same at 3/6d. Two additional garages were added to the range. A "Large-size Garage" mounted on a 19x14 inch board and comprising a double bay workshop bearing the sign "Astra Garage", oil bins and three illuminated petrol pumps. The fourth garage at 21/- was almost twice the price of the "Large size Garage" and must have been quite elaborate, but to date the author has not seen one. Model garages seen by the author, and illustrated here, differ in some details from those illustrated in Astra-Pharos catalogues and advertisements.

A set of 4 floodlights was introduced towards the end of the year; each floodlight was painted white and had a different coloured Perspex filter. The set included a substantial green painted battery holder, which incorporated a 4-position switch. Said to be "splendid for illuminating an aerodrome, dolls house, garage or other model building". The 4 floodlights could also be purchased in a box on their own without the battery holder.

Also produced at the end of 1936 were a motor ramp at 1/11d and a display board at 37/6d. The author has not seen either of these models, however the display board must have been a substantial toy as 37/6d was a lot of money in the mid 1930s.

The machine gun, introduced mid year, was a sign of things to come. This was 24 inches long and was mounted on a 22-inch high tripod. It fired rolls of caps by cranking a handle on the right hand side.

The Military Range

Mid 1937 saw the introduction of a new range of mostly military models. Only the 3-light traffic signal, the floodlighting set and a modified round based searchlight being carried over from the previous range. Each model was now assigned a number and this was to remain unchanged for as long as toy production continued. Unless otherwise described, all models in this range were painted the colour khaki until late 1938 when the colour was changed to dark green.

Model Number 1 was a "miniature 3 way traffic signal" standing 4½ inches high. The signal, which was painted black with 3 white bands around the column, was mounted at one end of a 4¾ inch oblong plate. Behind the signal was an oblong battery box painted silver, with the red Astra rounded mounted in its centre. The on/off screw switch was mounted at the rear of the battery box, and the control for the light sequence mounted on the back of the signal behind the bulbs. (C)

Model Number 2 was a "miniature 6-light traffic signal". This was similar in dimensions and operation to model number 1, but the battery box was painted cream. (C)

Model Number 3 was the standard 7¾ inch high "3 light traffic signal" carried over from the previous range. It was painted black as before, but now with 3 white rings around the column. (C)

Model Number 4 was in fact two models, a single barrel and a double barrel sporting gun/rifle. These were the first models to incorporate the newly patented "cartridge for firing projectiles from toy firearms". The guns were 33 inches in overall length and hinged at the breech to load the brass shell case. This case was in two parts, which separated so as to insert a cap (amorces). The case was then screwed back together and a wooden "bullet" inserted at one end. The case was then loaded into the breech and the gun was ready to fire. The gases produced from the exploding cap forcing the "bullet" down the barrel. (E)

Model Number 5 was an anti-aircraft gun with a 5-inch barrel mounted on a triangular base. An Astra roundel was fixed to one of the triangular legs. The elevation could be changed and fixed by tightening a chrome-plated screw on the left-hand side. The gun was fired using the same detachable brass shell case as model number 4. This model appears to have been very successful, priced at 4/6d and is one of the most commonly found Astra toys today. (A)

Model Number 6 was a "glider launching deck" and consisted of an oblong deck 14 inches long supported on 4 feet together with a glider. The plane had a 5-inch wingspan and the word ASTRA in capitals across the wing. (E)

Model Number 7 was an "anti-aircraft station". This consisted of a wooden board 12x9 inches painted mid green together with two anti-aircraft guns (model 5) and one standard searchlight (model 14-described later), which could be mounted anywhere on the board. (E)

Model Number 8 was the "floodlight set" carried over from the previous range. (D)

Model Number 9 was a "mobile anti-aircraft gun". This was the model 5 anti-aircraft gun with the triangular base drilled to accept 4 wheels. The wheel centres were nickel-plated and drilled with 6 holes and were mounted with smooth grey rubber tyres. (C)

Model Number 10 was a "mobile searchlight". This used the triangular base with 4 wheels from the previous model and mounted the new lamp from the round based searchlight (model 15) in place of the anti-aircraft gun. Turning a chrome-plated knob mounted on the side could alter the elevation of this new searchlight. The battery was stored in a box mounted between the two widely spaced wheels. (D)

Model Number 11 was a "searchlight on an 'O' gauge railway truck". The base of the truck and the wheels were die-cast and the flat bed was a polished aluminium sheet. The searchlight, taken from the miniature searchlight (model 16 described later) was mounted in the centre of the flat bed and the Astra roundel fixed on the bed in front of it. A battery clip was mounted underneath the model. (D)

Model Number 12 was a "mobile unit". This consisted of a die-cast base 12 inches long with an axle mounted with 2 wheels (identical to those used in model 9 and 10) at either end. The searchlight with screw adjustable elevation was mounted at one end; the anti-aircraft gun from model 5 was mounted in the middle and an ammunition box, covered with polished aluminium sheet moulded into the other end. The Astra roundel was mounted on a screw which held the aluminium box cover in place and a battery clip was fixed on the underside of the model. (D)

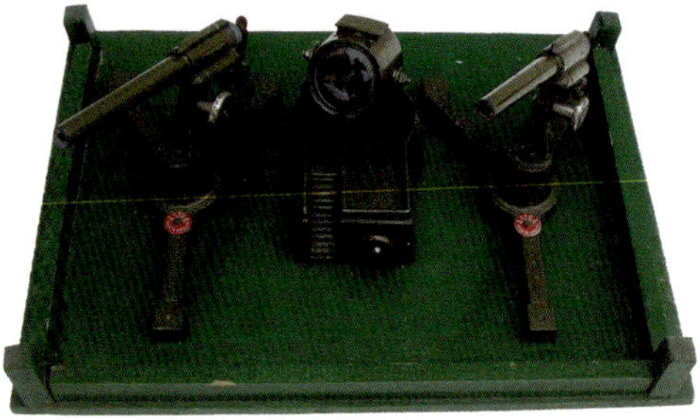

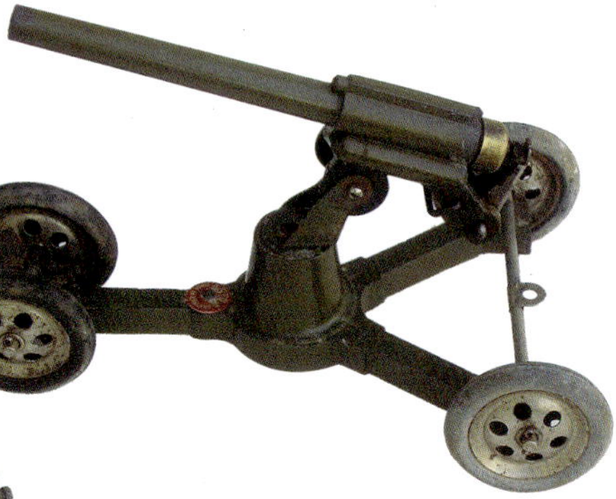

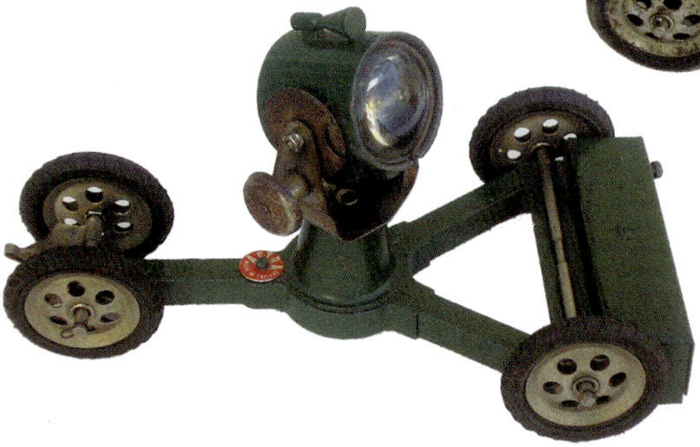

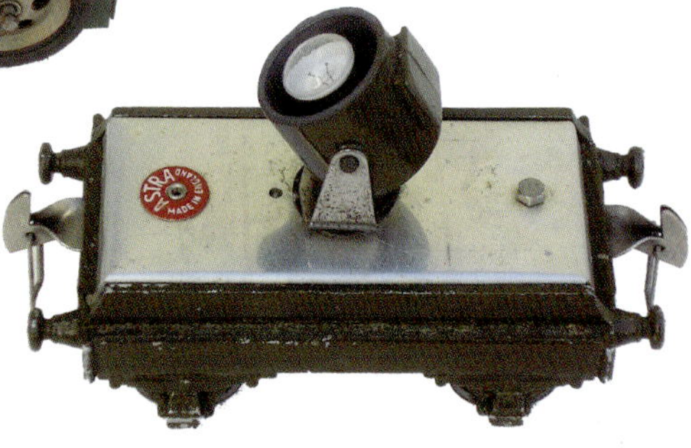
ASTRA

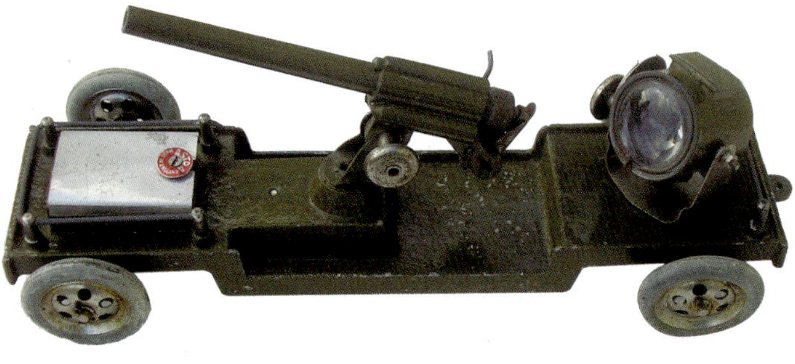

Model Number 13 was a "super searchlight". This stood 8 inches high and had a 4-inch diameter projector. A wheel attached to the side controlled elevation. The Astra roundel was fixed to the conical die-cast base and the battery mounted underneath. (D)

Model Number 14 was a "standard searchlight". The base was approximately oblong with steps cast into the rear left hand side. The projector swivelled and elevated but did not have the fine control mechanism, which was fitted to the roundbased searchlight. The battery was mounted underneath the base (B). A pair of these searchlights modified for Morse signalling was also offered. (E)

Model Number 15 was the "round base searchlight". This model was carried over from the previous range, but had an improved projector casting with screw controlled elevation. Although the projector was the same as that used on the "standard searchlight", this model gave a more powerful light because it had a more powerful bulb and a 4½ volt battery.
The round base searchlight was in production for longer than any other model and as a consequence is the most common Astra toy found today. (A)

Model Number 16 was the "miniature searchlight". Standing only 2¼ inches high, this was the smallest searchlight that Astra produced. The projector was a smaller version of that used on the "standard searchlight". It swivelled and elevated in a similar way and was mounted on an oblong base which was too small to contain the battery. (B)

Model Number 17 was the "12 inch heavy howitzer". This beautifully made gun was 10½ inches long and had a 7¼ inch barrel which could be elevated by turning a screw on the left hand side. On the right hand side of the barrel was a sighting telescope. The gun was fired using brass shell cases similar to models 4 and 5. However the shell cases for the howitzer were of larger diameter and used hard rubber "bullets" instead of small diameter wooden ones. (C)

Model Number 18 was the magnificent "3.7 Anti Aircraft Gun". This was the model most people associate with Astra-Pharos, since it featured prominently in their advertising over many years. The gun had a large 9-inch barrel and weighed almost 4lb. It had a range finding dial and gear operated traverse and elevation controls. It fired using the same detachable brass shell case as Model Number 4 and had quite a realistic breech mechanism.

It was first produced at the end of 1938/ beginning of 1939 even though it was included in the 1938 price list and marked a change of colour for Astra military models which up until now had been painted Khaki. From this date onwards the models were painted dark green. (C)

Model Number 19 was a rare "Anti Aircraft gun", standing just over 4 inches high and mounted on a heavy round conical base, which also supported the Astra roundel. Its barrel was a similar casting to that of Anti Aircraft gun model number 5 and it elevated in a similar way but it had a unique breech and firing mechanism. A wooden bullet was loaded into the open breech and a cap was placed in a recess just below. The flat breechblock was then closed and held in place by a flat spring mounted along the top of the barrel. A separate firing hammer was then used to strike a firing pin projecting from the breechblock. These models were only produced for a short period from the end of 1937 until early 1938. They were not shown in the 1939 price list.   (E)

Model Number 20 was a "gun on truck". This was a simple cap firing gun mounted on the same 'O' gauge railway track base as model number 11. The barrel was a new casting 3¾ inches long and had a pin sized hole drilled at the breech end. The wooden bullet was loaded from the muzzle and a cap placed over the pinhole at the breech. A firing hammer then struck the cap and the gases produced forced the bullet up the barrel. This barrel and firing mechanism were to be used in a range on subsequent models.   (D)

Model Number 21 was the "fort gun". This consisted of the barrel and breech mechanism from model number 20 mounted on the "standard searchlight" base. This model was to remain in production for many years, but with different barrel castings and different base mountings. (A)

Model Number 22 was the very large "¼-mile beam searchlight". The 4-inch diameter projector working off 9-volt batteries produced a very powerful beam of light. The beam could be elevated and traversed by means of control wheel mounted on the two rods out to one side.

The base detail of these models produced during the war was much finer than the rather crude castings produced post war.   (B)

Model Number 23 the "light anti-aircraft gun" was new to the model range for 1940. This consisted of the gun barrel from model number 20 mounted on a light cast tripod base.   (D)

Model Number 24 was the "anti-tank gun". This attractive model was produced in large numbers and consisted of a cast base supported on an axle with twin rubber tyred wheels at either end. A protective vertical steel shield was mounted on the base with a new barrel casting protruding through it. The firing mechanism was identical to that of model number 20 and elevation was achieved via an elevation screw mounted at the rear of the base casting.   (A)

No. 13

No. 14

No. 14
Morse Signal

*

No. 15

No. 16

No. 17

No. 20

No. 21

No. 22

No. 23

No. 24

27

Model 24 was the last new model to be produced until after the war, but several model variations worth noting were produced at this time.

The fort gun model number 21 was fitted to a new base which looked like a gun emplacement mounted in rocks.

Due to the shortage of brass the patented brass shell case used in model number 5, 9 and 12 could not be produced, so the barrel casting was modified at the breech to incorporate a cap mounting platform with a pinhole in the middle so that the models could be fired using the same principle as model number 20. At the same time the cast base of the "mobile unit" model number 12 was changed to a new design, which avoided using aluminium. Except for the fort gun, models showing these design changes are rare.

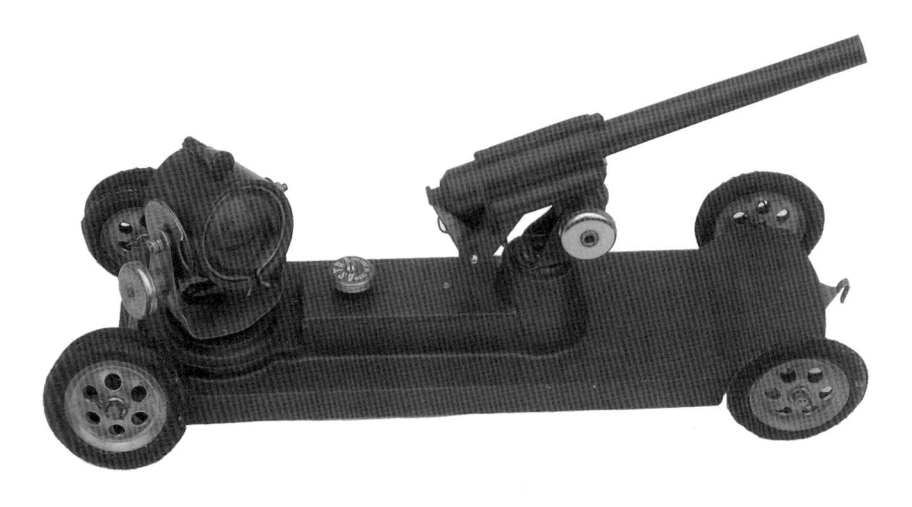

Post War Toys

The Astra advertisement in the Meccano Magazine of November 1945 announced that limited supplies of toys were now available. Model numbers 5, 15, 17, 18, 21, 22 and 24 were offered, although the heavy howitzer was soon discontinued. The round-based searchlight was now cast from the wartime mould in a light alloy and painted a pale green. All new models, which began with the pom-pom gun in 1946, were cast in light alloy and painted light green, but the other wartime models were still painted dark green.

Model Number 25 was the "pom-pom gun". This was based on the naval twin barred oerlikon gun and was spring operated. It had an overall length of 10 inches and would fire single shots or a stream of projectiles, with the barrels recoiling after each shot, when the side mounted handle was turned. Ammunition was contained in a magazine mounted at the breech end of the barrels. The cover for the magazine had the patent number stamped on it. (C)

Model Number 26 was a "new Anti-Aircraft gun". This all new model was cast in light alloy and was a cross between the number 5 A.A gun and the beautifully detailed number 18 A.A gun. It used the two piece brass shell case and caps to fire the new plastic projectiles or this could be replaced with a one-piece aluminium shell case of similar dimensions. The plastic projectile protruded through the base of this new shell case and the force of the hammer blow striking the case drove the projectiles down the barrel. Traversing the barrel was a manual operation, but elevation was by means of a turn screw. (D)

Model Number 27 was the "rocket gun". This six-barrelled gun was loosely based on the German Second World War rocket launcher. It was mounted on the anti-tank gun base and had an elevation screw mounted to one side. The internal barrel springs were depressed by means of a plunger supplied with the gun, and the alloy rockets dropped down the 6 barrels (with or without a cap stuck to the base). The gun was then fired by pressing one of the three levers at the rear of the barrels. Light pressure fired the top barrel whilst heavier pressure fired the bottom one. (B)

Model Number 28 was the "miniature searchlight". This all-new 3¼ inch high searchlight was cast in light alloy and had an elevating and traversing arm mounted to the side (in a similar way to the ¼ mile beam searchlight). The 3 volt battery was mounted in the base.

This was the first model to be produced in the all white boxes with a green illustration of the model on the side. The model has "Astra" cast into the base and does not carry the usual Astra roundel. (C)

Model Number 29 was a "3 light traffic signal". This was the first of four signals to be introduced during 1949/1950. It had a pale green base, which housed the battery and a black column with 3 white rings around it. On top of the column a black oval head housed red, amber and green lenses. The switching mechanism was mounted at the back of the head. (C)

Model Number 33 was the "6 light traffic signal". This 6 inch high model used the same base and column as the 3 light signal, but used an angular 6 light head. The light sequence was obtained by operating a lever at the back of the head. (C)

Model Number 40 was the "4 light railway signal". This 5½ inch high model shared no components with number 29 or number 33. The pale green base and black column were different castings with a black oval head containing the red, amber, amber and green lenses. The 4½ volt battery was mounted in the base and light sequence was obtained by operating a 4-position lever on the right hand side of the base. There are two different versions of this model, the earliest version has 4 bulbs (one for each coloured light), the later type has just one bulb which swivels in front of each coloured lens in turn. (D)

Model Number 42 was the "miniature signal". This 4 inch high model used the base of the miniature searchlight, model number 28, fitted with a slim black column and a black 2 light head. Operating a lever at the rear of the head illuminated the red and green lenses. This model had no Astra roundel. (D)

The author knows of no reason why the numbering system for the last three models is out of sequence. Three new models were introduced in 1952 and these do not appear to have been assigned a model number at all.

32

New Anti Tank Gun

This model used the cut down base of the old anti tank gun (model 24) with a pair of rear facing, pressed aluminium trials mounted on either side of the protective side of the shield. The twin wheels were replaced with large single solid rubber wheels. The barrel and firing mechanism were the same as on model 24, but a flash eliminator was fitted to the end of the barrel. The gun was painted dark green. (D)

Car Hoist

On this 3 inch high model, two red painted car ramps are raised by operating a lever mounted on the rounded section behind the lifting post. The lifting post and mechanism cover were painted dark green or pale blue. (D)

Coronation Chair

This model, introduced for the 1953 Coronation, was 2¾ inches high and painted gold with red chair arms. It had a pencil sharpener in the base of the chair with the access hole on the right hand side, looking from the front of the chair. There are no markings on this model to identify it as made by Astra-Pharos. (D)

Model Variations

2 Inch Diameter Searchlight

The first version of this model was cast in aluminium alloy and painted charcoal grey. The quality of casting of the lamp unit was poor, but the base was much better. A rather ineffective copper spring, with a single mounting point, made contact with the rear of the bulb as it protruded through the rear of the lamp unit. A roughly square section at the rear of the base was cut away and a stiff black card riveted behind the hole. Mounted on the card, by means of a rivet, was the simple copper on/off lever. On the front of the base was a black and silver oval with the words "Astra British Made".

The second version used a much improved aluminium casting for the lamp holder, but had a cast iron base. The model changed colour to battleship grey except for the 'U' shaped bracket supporting the lamp unit, which was painted black. The contact with the rear of the bulb was much improved and consisted of a copper contact soldered on to a black steel strip secured to the lamp holder with 2 rivets. The on/off switch was a simple screw down handle mounted on the upper left rear corner of the base.

The final version was very similar to the previous one except that the 'U' shaped bracket supporting the lamp unit was lower in height and painted grey. The on/off switch had moved to a slot cut in the left-hand side of the top the base. Here a simple lever pushed back and forward for on and off. The black and silver oval label now read "Astra London Made"

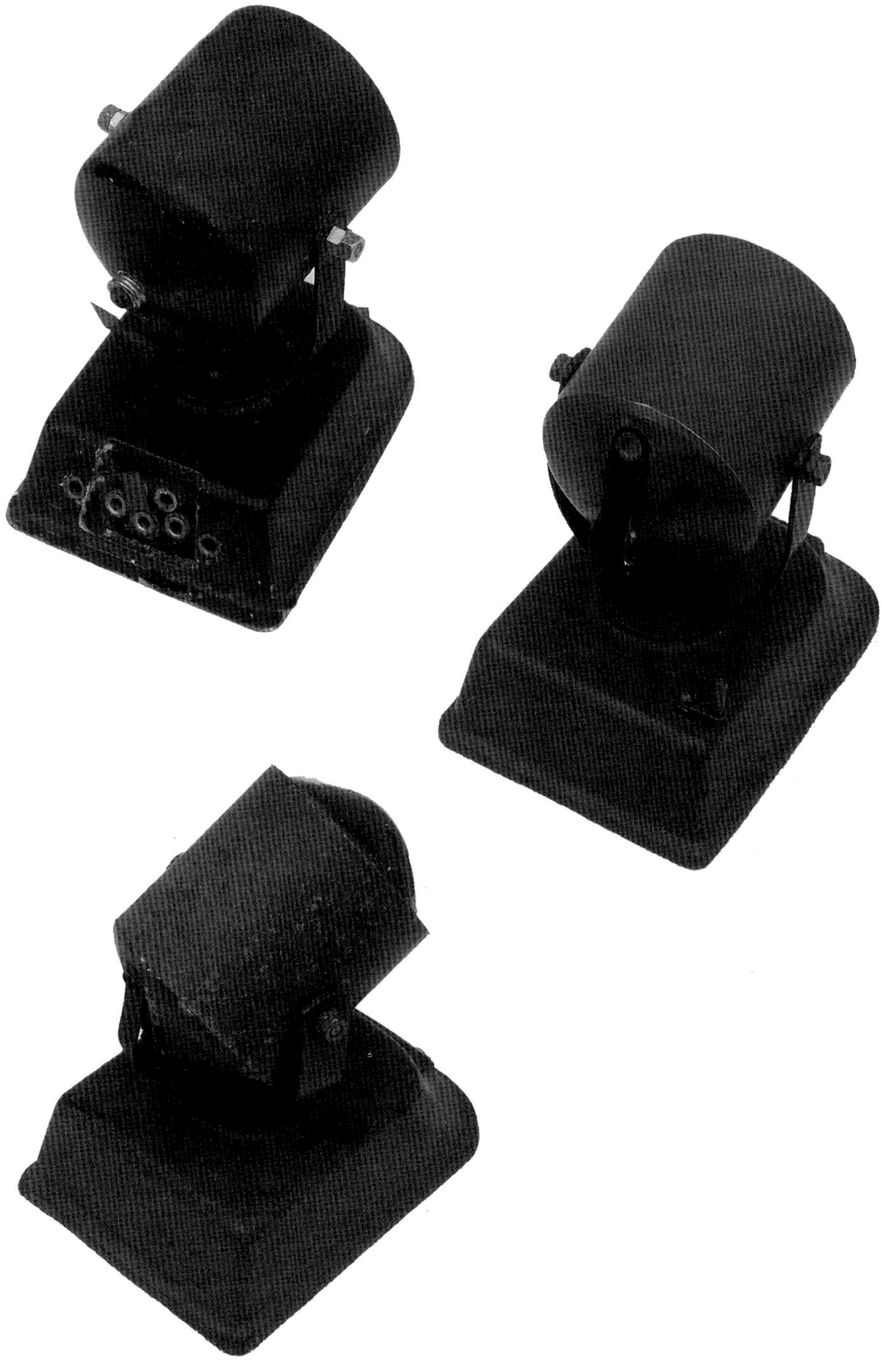

*

Round Based Searchlight

This model had the longest production run of all the Astra toys. It was introduced in 1933 and had a heavy cast iron round base with 5 steps leading up to the 1¼ inch diameter searchlight. The searchlight was supported on a simple narrow 'U' shaped frame, and the model was painted battleship grey. This first model was short lived, and the searchlight casting was modified with an oblong flat area cast into the top. The 'U' shaped frame was widened considerably and 2 round holes punched in each side. The whole model was painted grey.

By 1937 the model was painted Khaki and the searchlight had a new 'U' shaped mounting frame. This frame incorporated a "fine control" friction mechanism for elevation and depression. The rest of the model was unchanged.

In 1938 the model sported a new searchlight casting with an imitation cooling fan cast onto the top in place of the flat area. The following year the model changed colour to dark green and the 5 supports for the handrail were altered which had the effect of lowering the rail.

The next change was a new slightly altered mould for the round base, but the castings from it were made of a lighter alloy not iron. The 5 supports for the handrail were changed again. The lower height was maintained but a hexagonal nut was placed at the base of each support.

The next model was still painted dark green, but now the round base was stamped out of sheet steel and had much less detail. By the late 1940s the model changed colour to light green. The base was still sheet steel, but the searchlight was now cast in an aluminium alloy making the whole model much lighter. The Astra roundel was moved from the back of the light on to the front on/off screw mounted on the side of the base. The hexagonal nuts on the handrail supports were replaced with dome shaped mounts.

The final light green 1950s version was produced from new moulds for the base and the lamp. These produced a finely detailed toy cast in aluminium alloy. The Astra roundel moved back to the back of the light again.

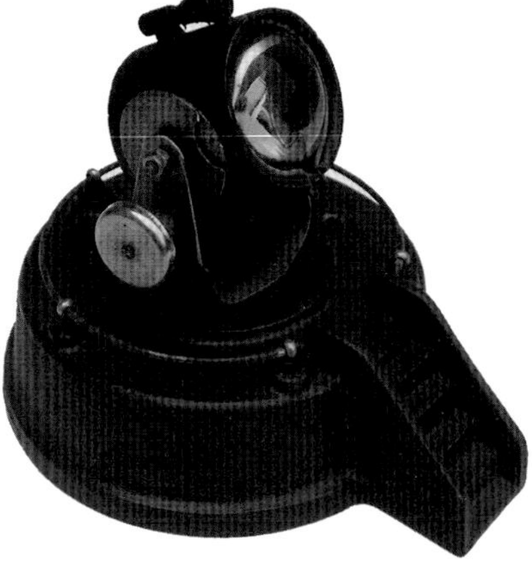
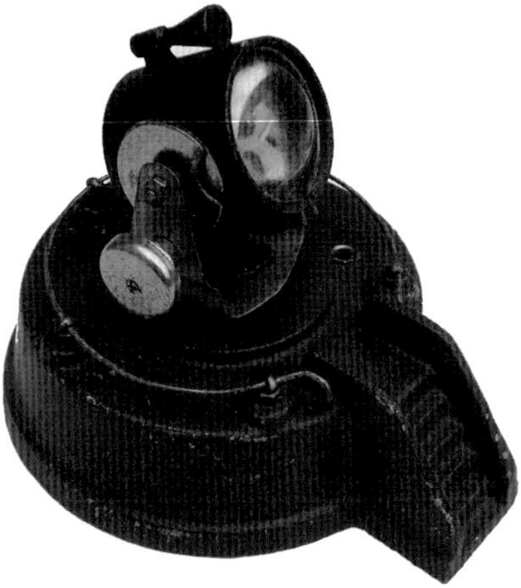
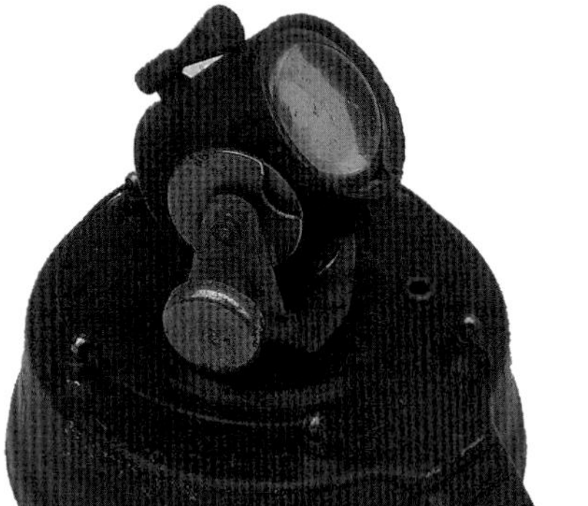
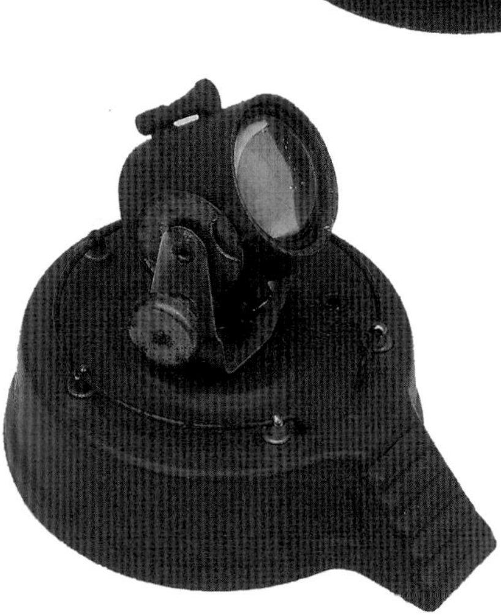
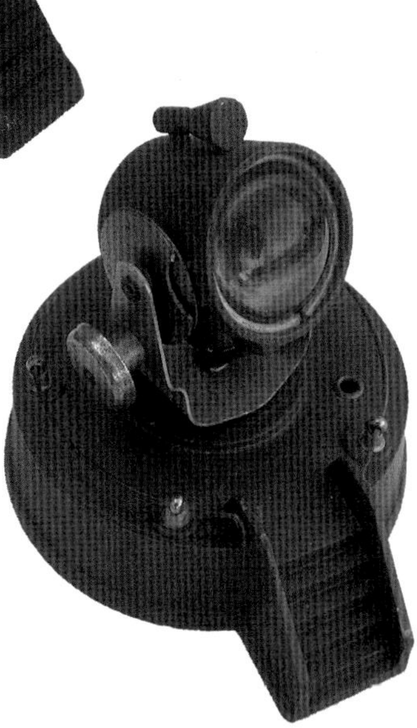

The Fort Gun

This was introduced in 1938/1939 and at first shared the gun barrel and mounts with the "gun on a railway truck". The gun was mounted on the cast iron standard searchlight base. This variation was short lived and 1940 introduced an all new model.

The new model had a gun mounted in a cast iron cupola. The gun barrel was painted dark green and was identical to that used in model number 23, the light Anti-Aircraft Gun. It was mounted on a separate sheet steel base. The realistic cupola was painted steel grey and had 4 full width steps at the rear.

The final version was produced in the late 1940's. The cupola, which was painted grey/green, was cast in an aluminium alloy and lost much of its fine detail. The gun was a short barrelled version of the "Anti Tank Gun" and was painted dark green.

The Heavy Howitzer

This was introduced mid 1937 and was painted khaki. The impressive gun barrel was 7¼ inches long and was made in two parts. The rear 3¼ inches being cast iron into which was sleeved a brass tube, which formed the rest of the barrel. The muzzle of the gun had a slight flare.

By 1939 the colour had changed to dark green and the brass tube had been replaced with steel one, which lost the flared muzzle.

During 1940/41 the gun was replaced with a short barrelled version. This dark green gun was identical in all other respects with its predecessors, but the barrel was now a one piece casting 5¼ inches in length. It remained in production until the late 1940s.

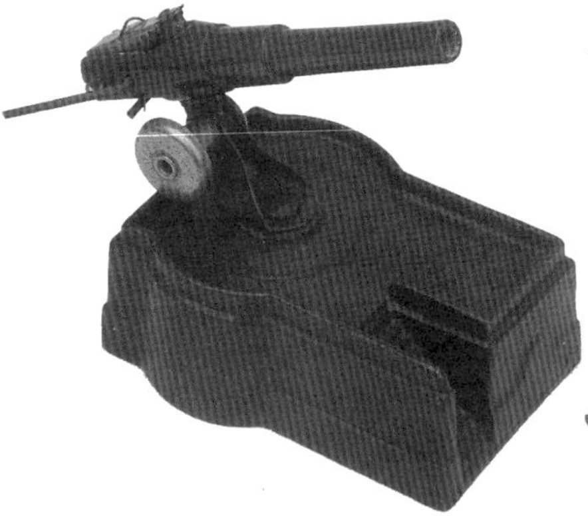

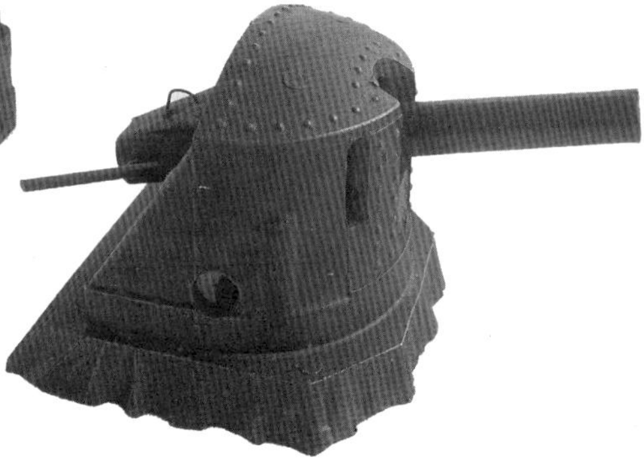

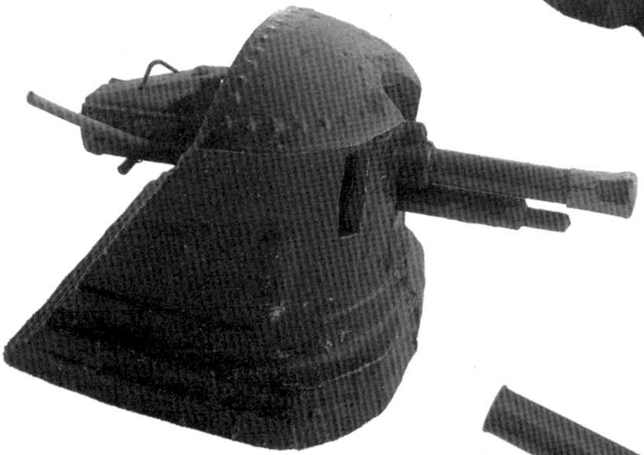

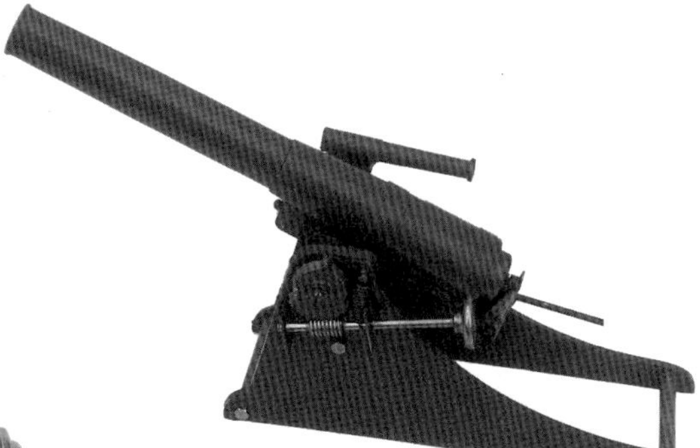

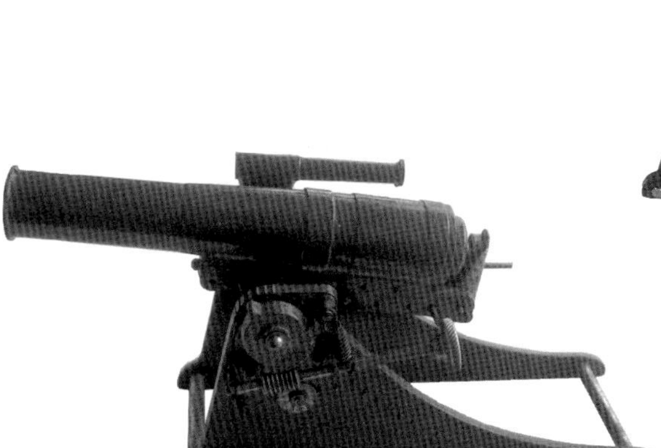

¼ Mile Beam Searchlight

Three varieties of this model exist.

Pre war models were dark green and had cast iron bases and lamp supports. The detail was fine, with the flat base behind the lamp patterned with fine lines forming diamond shapes. The concentric circles behind the glass of the light were painted black.

The post war model was more crudely cast in aluminium alloy. The flat base behind the lamp had raised bumps like cobbles and the concentric circles behind the glass were unpainted aluminium. Earlier models were painted the same dark green as pre war models and used the same rod mechanism and connectors to control the light.
By the 1950s the colour had changed to light green and the rod mechanism was shortened slightly. The oblong block connecting the 2 rods was removed and the end of the lower rod was twisted round the upper one to make the connection.

The Rocket Gun

There were several versions of this model, which was introduced in 1948. Early models used a pair of twin wheels, identical to those used on the anti tank gun and were painted light green.

By 1952 the same model was painted dark green.

The very last advertisement that Astra-Pharos took out in Meccano Magazine in January 1954 shows a new version of the Rocket Gun with the block of 6 barrels mounted on the base of the "new anti tank gun", using the pair of large solid rubber wheels and twin trials from that model. This was painted a much darker green than any of the previous models. A simpler version was also produced without the twin trials.

Two other versions exist based on the original 1948 model. The first was painted in the very dark green and used very small twin wheels. The second version was painted light green, but with a pair of solid rubber wheels, which have a course tread pattern cast across the face of the wheel. The same wheels were used by Astra-Johilco from about 1955 and it is difficult to know which manufacturer produced this model.

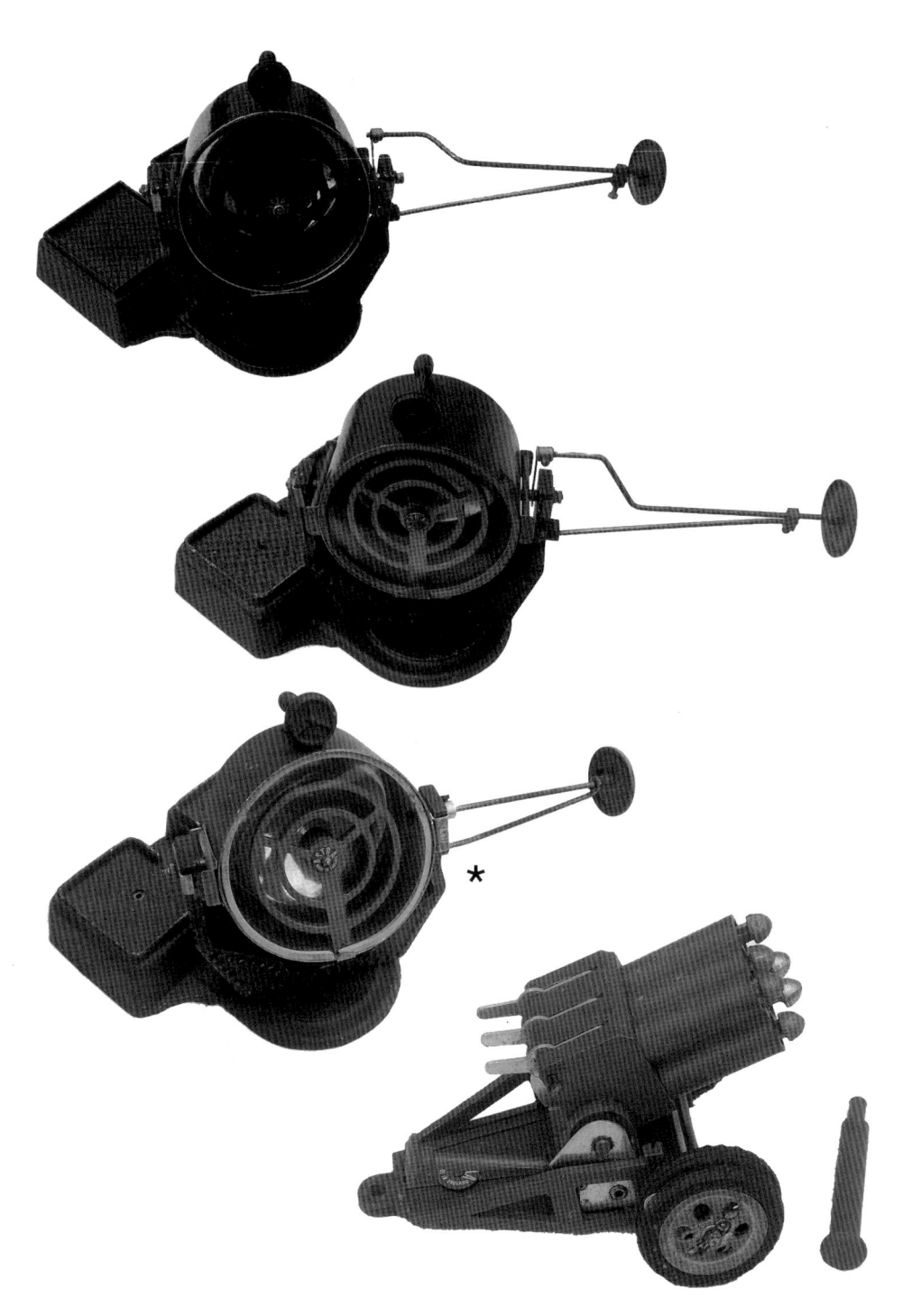

*

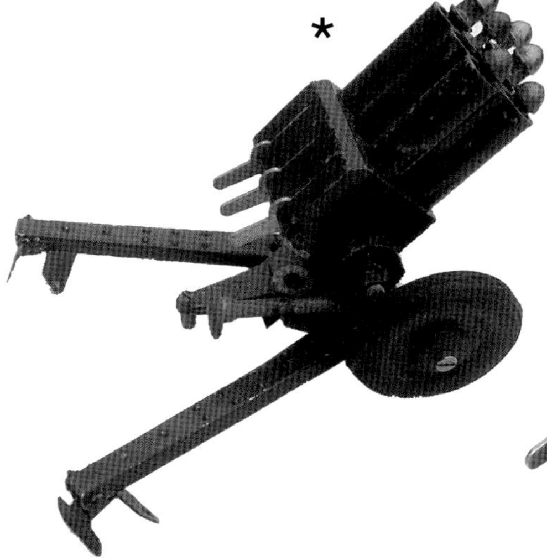
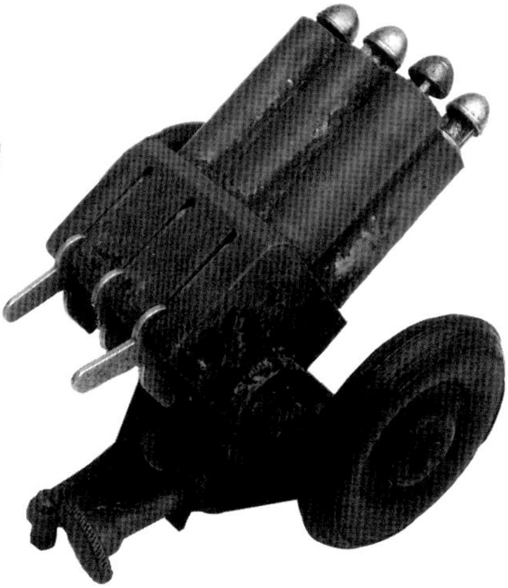
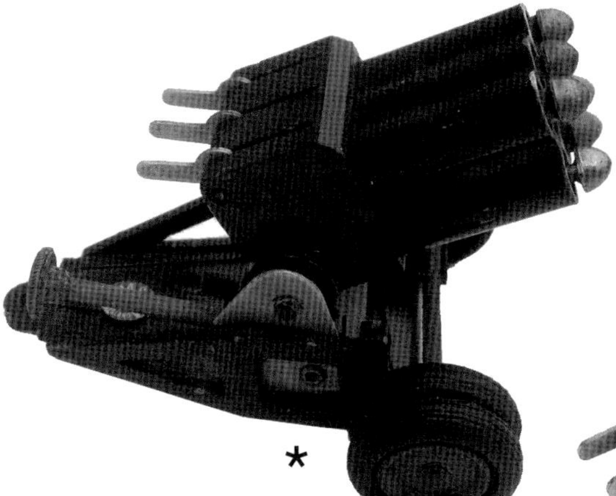
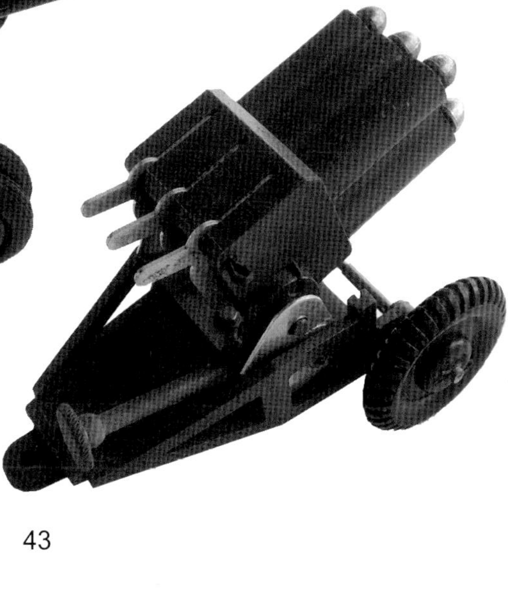

Astra Johillco and Wend-al Astra

in 1954/1955 Astra-Pharos sold some of their toy making moulds to Johillco and Wend-al Toys. These two companies then produced a small range of toys which were very similar to those made by Astra-Pharos. To compound the confusion, both companies initially sold their products in original Astra-Pharos boxes (presumably purchased at the same time as the toy moulds).

Astra Johillco

Of the two companies, Johillco produced the better quality toys and introduced a 6 model range. Initially using old Astra-Pharos boxes, they soon introduced their own distinctively illustrated box. The dark green base colour on all the model guns was lightly over sprayed with brown in places to simulate camouflage.

Light Anti Aircraft Gun

This used the base of the number 26 anti aircraft gun and attached a modified anti tank gun barrel and breech to it. The breech casting was altered to produce a small "flash protector" on each side of the cap firing area. Elevation was by means of a small wheel on the right hand side with manual traverse. Painted dark green and silver.

Anti Tank Gun

This was very similar to the "New Anti Tank Gun", using the pair of single wheels. The barrel and breech were the same modified casting as used on the anti aircraft gun. Painted dark green and silver.

A second version of this gun has been seen with a pair of single wheels which had a coarse tread pattern.

Mobile Gun

This was the same model as the anti tank gun but with smaller plastic wheels and no trails. Painted dark green and silver.

Rocket Gun

This was based on the last Astra-Pharos version using the carriage of the "New Anti Tank Gun" and had a pair of single wheels and pressed aluminium trails. Painted dark green.

Searchlight

This used the base of the model 29/33 traffic signal and attached the projector from the round based searchlight. The searchlight elevation mechanism was identical to the Astra product. Painted light green.

Miniature Searchlight

This was identical to the Astra model number 28. Painted light green.

46

Wend-al Astra

In general, these models were crudely cast in aluminium alloy and were painted matt khaki. They retained the red Astra roundel and were sold in buff coloured boxes with Astra-Pharos labels. Occasionally a "Wend-al Toys" label was also fixed to the boxes.

3.7 Anti Aircraft Gun

This was a simplified version of the Astra-Pharos product using the original mould. Traverse was manual, but elevation was by a crude wheel and gear device mounted on the right hand side. The gun came with a brass two piece shell case for use with caps, and an aluminium shell case identical to that supplied with model number 26.

Mobile Gun

This was almost identical to the Astra Johillco product using the same barrel casting with the modified breech area. The small wheels were rubber with 3 grooves running round them.

Fort Gun

This used the same barrel and breech as the mobile gun, but had a unique cupola. The cupola was much smaller than the Astra Pharos product and cast with no detail on the outside but still had two small forward facing view slots.

Searchlight

This used the base of the model 29/33 traffic signal and attached a crudely cast projector from the round based searchlight supported on a cast 'U' shaped frame. The searchlight elevation mechanism was replaced with a spoked locking wheel painted silver.

48

49

Anti Tank Gun

There were three versions of this model.

The first was very similar to the "New Anti Tank Gun" except that the trails were solid cast and not pressed aluminium. The single rubber wheels were the same as used on the Astra-Pharos model, and the barrel and breech used the modified anti tank gun casting. Painted matt khaki, some models were painted with desert group decals.

The second version was the same as the first except for the single wheels which had a coarse tread pattern.

The third version had very thin cast trails and used the same twin wheels as many early Astra-Pharos models. It used the unmodified Astra Pharos anti tank gun barrel.

Light Anti Aircraft Gun

This was a more crudely cast version of the Astra Johillco model, without the elevation wheel.

Boxes and Labels

The earliest boxes were made from buff coloured cardboard and had a simple white label attached with the words "ASTRA (registered)", "British Made" and the name of the model. For a limited time in this early period box lids and bases were coloured mid blue with a "cracked ice" pattern in gold printed on them. Once the "ASTRA" trade mark had been granted the box lids and bases were coloured matt pale grey/green and the white label changed to read "ASTRA trade mark", "Made in London, England" and the name of the model. The one exception being the 2 inch diameter searchlight box which had a white label with a black and white illustration of the model printed on it. These grey/green boxes can be deceptive, because in bright light they fade and take on a buff appearance. In about 1936 the box labels changed completely. They were now coloured blue, yellow and white and bore a new ASTRA logo in a diamond shape. This style and colour of labels remained unchanged until production of toys ceased.

When the new military range was introduced all the boxes were changed to a shiny light bright green. This green had darkened in colour by 1939. As supplies of green boxes dried up during the war, good quality buff coloured boxes were re-introduced.

Post war, the buff coloured boxes were continued with the pre war blue, yellow and white labels. However the quality of the cardboard used to make the boxes was poor. Astra-Pharos were successful in purchasing some empty boxes for war time gas masks and these were used for round based searchlights and number 5 anti aircraft guns with the usual Astra Labels attached.

Late 1940's early 1950's saw the introduction of a new style of box for the traffic and railway signal range and for the new miniature searchlight. These boxes were made of thin white cardboard with an illustration of the model on the box, together with the model name, the Astra logo and address and operating instructions all printed in green ink.

ASTRA
(Registered)
MODEL
SEARCH LIGHT.
British Made.

ASTRA
Trade Mark
MODEL
SEARCH LIGHT.
PERCY GOODWIN, LTD.

ASTRA
TRADE MARK
SIX LIGHT
ELECTRIC SIGNAL
Made in London, England.

This Box Contains
ONE
MODEL
12"
HEAVY
HOWITZER
ASTRA
ASTRA-PHAROS
This Box Contains
ONE
MODEL
ANTI-
AIRCRAFT
GUN
ASTRA
ASTRA-PHAROS

This Box Contains
ONE
MODEL
ANTI-
TANK
GUN
ASTRA
TRADE MARK
MADE IN LONDON ENGLAND
MANUFACTURERS
PATENTEES
Sole Distributors:
ASTRA-PHAROS
LIMITED
LANDOR WORKS:
ASKEW ROAD,
LONDON, W.12

BRITISH MADE TOYS OF QUALITY
ASTRA
TRADE MARK
MADE IN LONDON ENGLAND
MANUFACTURERS,
PATENTEES, AND
SOLE DISTRIBUTORS:
Astra-Pharos Ltd.
LANDOR WORKS:
ASKEW. ROAD, LONDON, W.12

ASTRA

ASTRA
JOHILLCO
ASTRA
JOHILLCO

Projectiles and Shell Cases

Projectiles and Shell Cases

The left hand side of the illustration on page 53, starting from the top, shows the brass shell case and wooden shell used with model numbers 4,5,7,9,12 and 18. Below this is the same shell case unscrewed to show the two halves. Underneath this is the much larger brass shell case used with the Heavy Howitzer and its hard rubber shell.

At the bottom left is the aluminium shell case which was included, as well as the brass type, with the New Anti Aircraft Gun model 26. The red and green plastic shells would protrude through the bottom of the shell case and when struck by the hammer of the gun would exit the barrel without having to use caps.

On the right of the illustration are two aluminium rockets from the Rocket Gun, and in-between these are two shells from the Pom Pom Gun. The pom pom shells are seven eighths of an inch long and made of aluminium rod rounded at one end.

Catalogues

The following pages show reproductions of the 1935, 1937, 1939, 1940, 1949 and 1950 catalogues of Astra-Pharos. The 1935 to 1940 catalogues were printed in red and black ink on off-white paper. The 1935 catalogue was printed in 3 blocks on both sides of a long strip of paper, and folded twice. The 1937, 1939 and 1940 catalogues were printed on both sides of a single sheet of paper. The 1937 catalogue was folded four times so that it would fit into a standard small envelope.

The 1949 catalogue was a more elaborate affair printed in red and black ink with all the models illustrated being coloured dark green. It measured 28 x 44 cm and the rather thick cream coloured paper was folded twice. The 1950 "Coloured Light Signals" catalogue was again printed in red and black but this time all the illustrated signals were coloured very pale green. The single sheet of white paper was printed on both sides and folded twice.

1937 Catalogue

WORKING MODELS AS SUPPLIED TO H.M. FORCES FOR TRAINING PURPOSES

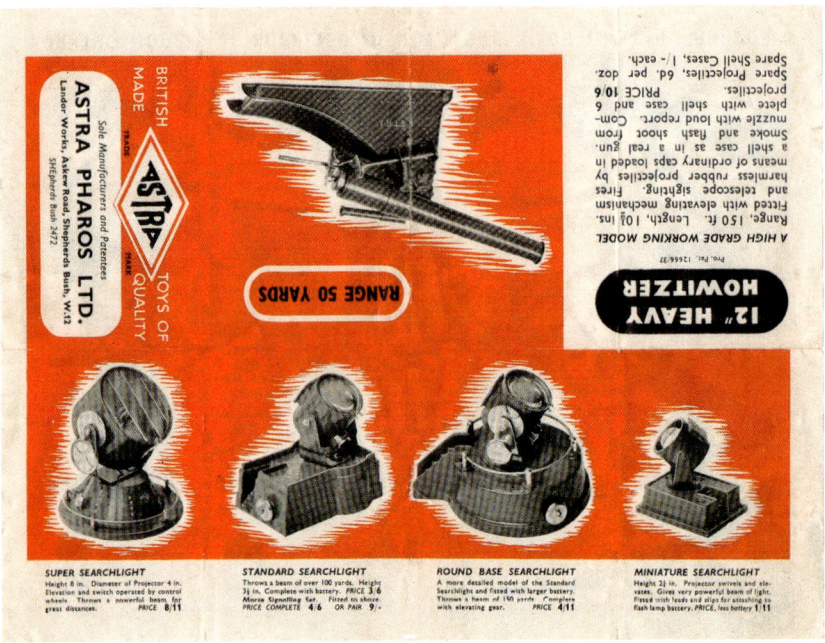

ASTRA PHAROS LTD.
Sole Manufacturers and Patentees
Lander Works, Askew Road, Shepherds Bush, W.12
Shepherds Bush 2472

BRITISH MADE — TOYS OF QUALITY

12" HEAVY HOWITZER
Pro. Pat. 12666/37

A HIGH GRADE WORKING MODEL
Range, 150 ft. Length, 10½ ins. Fitted with elevating mechanism and telescope sighting. Fires harmless rubber projectiles by means of ordinary caps loaded in a shell case as in a real gun. Smoke and flash shoot from muzzle with loud report. Complete with shell case and 6 projectiles.
PRICE 10/6
Spare Projectiles, 6d. per doz.
Spare Shell Cases, 1/- each.

RANGE 50 YARDS

1. **MINIATURE 3-WAY SIGNAL** — Overall height 4½ in. Switch controls red, amber and green lights. PRICE, with battery 3/6
2. **MINIATURE 6-Light SIGNAL** — Similar dimensions as the 3-Light. Illustrated at No. 1. PRICE, with battery 4/6
3. **3-LIGHT TRAFFIC SIGNAL** — Height 7½ in. Complete with battery. Switch controls Red, Amber and Green lights. Black finish. PRICE 2/11
4. **D.B. SPORTING GUN** — Pro. Patent 12666/37. Length 33 in. Fires harmless bullets (no license required). Range 50 yards. Complete with 2 cartridge cases and 6 dozen bullets. PRICE 15/11. Cartridge cases 9d. each. Bullets 6d. per dozen.
5. **SPORTING & TARGET RIFLE** — Pro. Patent 12666/37. Length 33 in. Fires harmless bullets (no license required). Range 50 yards. Complete with cartridge case and 6 dozen bullets. PRICE 8/11. Spare cartridge cases 9d. each. Bullets 6d. per dozen. These guns and rifles fire on the same principle as the 12 in. Howitzer overleaf.
6. **ANTI-AIRCRAFT GUN** — Pro. Patent 12666/37. Height 6½ in. Length of barrel 5 in. Fires projectiles (by means of caps) with great power and accuracy. Flash and smoke discharge and loud report. PRICE, complete with shell case and 12 projectiles 4/6
7. **GLIDER LAUNCHING DECK** — Pat. pending. With super crash proof Glider. The most efficient gliding apparatus on the market. Wonderful flights guaranteed. Length of deck 14 in., glider span 7½ in. PRICE, complete with instructions 2/6
8. **ANTI-AIRCRAFT STATION** — Pro. Patent 12666/37. The Station is mounted with two A.A. guns and Standard Searchlight. Size 12 × 9 in. PRICE complete 12/6
9. **FLOODLIGHTING SET** — Comprising four floodlights, fitted with different coloured lights, battery, battery holder and switch gear to operate each light. PRICE 7/6
10. **MOBILE ANTI-AIRCRAFT GUN** — Pro. Patent 12666/37. As described for No. 5. On special chassis with detachable rubber tyred wheels. PRICE complete 6/6
11. **MOBILE SEARCHLIGHT** — Fitted with the standard projector. Mounted on special chassis as above. Complete with battery. PRICE 6/6
12. **SEARCHLIGHT ON "O" GAUGE RAILWAY TRACK** — A necessity for every up-to-date model railway. Comprises high grade truck and powerful searchlight. Very strongly made of die-cast metal and aluminium. Perfect scale model, complete with switch and battery. Standard couplings. PRICE 4/11
13. **MOBILE UNIT** — Mounted with A.A. gun and standard searchlight. Length overall 12 in. An extremely well made model. PRICE, complete with battery and projectiles for gun 12/6

SUPER SEARCHLIGHT — Height 8 in. Diameter of Projector 4 in. Elevation and switch operated by control wheels. Throws a powerful beam for great distances. PRICE 8/11

STANDARD SEARCHLIGHT — Throws a beam of over 100 yards. Height 3½ in. Complete with battery. Morse Signalling fact. PRICE 3/6. PRICE ON SHOW COMPLETE 4/6 OR PAIR 9/-

ROUND BASE SEARCHLIGHT — A more detailed model of the Standard Searchlight and fitted with larger battery. Throws a beam of 140 yards. Complete with elevating gear. PRICE 4/11

MINIATURE SEARCHLIGHT — Height 2½ in. Projector swivels and sinuates. Gives very powerful beam of light. Fitted with leads and plugs for attaching to flash lamp battery. PRICE, less battery 1/11

56

1935 Catalogue

ELECTRICAL TOYS

SEARCHLIGHTS

A really well made model at a reasonable price. Stands 5 inches high. Throws a powerful beam of light adjustable through any angle, complete with switch and flash lamp battery housed in base, finished Battleship Grey.

Price **3/11**

CIRCULAR BASE SEARCHLIGHT, a more detailed model of the above, stands 4½ in. high, very powerful.

Price **5/6**

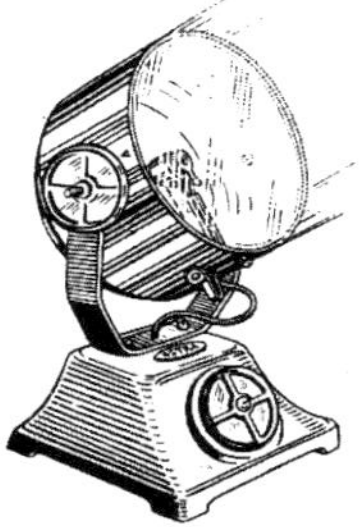

SUPER SEARCHLIGHTS

A beautifully made and imposing model. Height 8 in. Diameter of projector 5 in., focussing adjustment, elevation and switch operated by control wheels. Throws a powerful beam for great distances, supplied complete with battery, finished Battleship Grey.

Price **10/6**

TRADE MARK

ASTRA

LONDON MADE

Toys and Models

FROM **G. GREINER & Co.**

Offices: 10 & 12, Milton Street, Cripplegate, London

Warehouse: 1, HANOVER COURT, MILTON STREET, LONDON

57

1935 Catalogue

ELECTRICAL TOYS

FLOODLIGHT

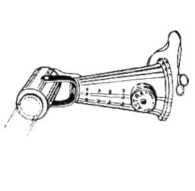

Floodlight throws a powerful beam; complete with leads for fixing to flash lamp battery, finish Battleship Grey.

Price **1/6**

MODEL HARBOUR

An attractive model for waterline ships, attractively finished, complete with leads for fixing to flash lamp battery.

Price **5/11**

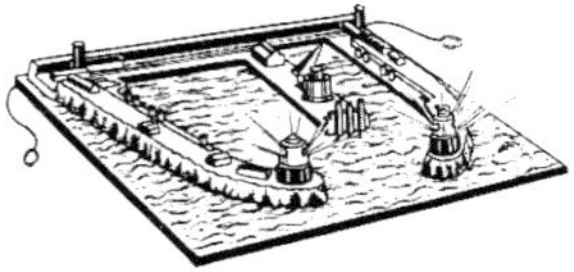

PIER HEAD AND BANDSTAND

A most realistic model, complete with Switch and Battery housed in base, lights up Bandstand and Pavilion.

Price **5/11**

ASTRA

LIGHTHOUSE, height 6½ in. complete with battery housed in stem and switch. Gives intermittent flashes, attractively finished in Buff, Green and Russet.

Price **3/11**

PETROL PUMP, height 6 in. complete with battery housed in stem. Rubber tubing and switch, Red finish.

Price **3/6**

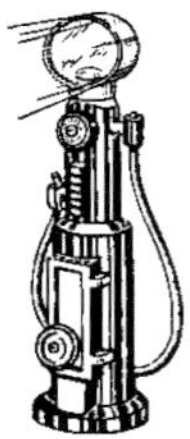

TRAFFIC SIGNALS

SIX - LIGHT Traffic Signal, height 6¾ in., complete with battery housed in stem, and switch controlling Red, Amber, Green, Amber, Green and Red Lights, black finish.

Price **4/11**

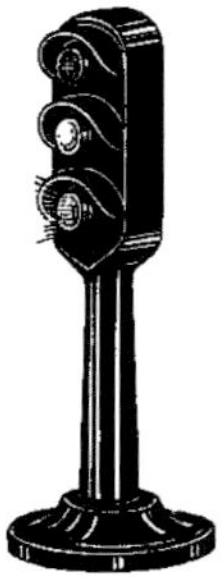

THREE-LIGHT Traffic Signal, height 7¾ in., complete with battery housed in stem, switch at back controls Red, Amber and Green Lights, Black finish.

Price **3/9**

TWO - LIGHT Railway or Traffic Signal, height 6¾ in. complete with battery housed in stem and switch controlling Red and Green Lights, Black finish.

Price **2/11**

1935 Catalogue

ASTRA TOYS

MORSE SIGNALLING SET

Height with tripod 22 in., diameter of projector 2½ in., a high grade practical set complete with two projectors with detachable tripods, and self contained batteries, effective for several miles in clear weather.

Finish Battleship Grey.

Price **12/6**

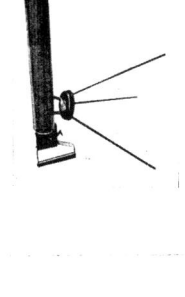

MACHINE GUN

A most realistic model 24 in. long, standing on a collapsible tripod 22 in. high, fires rolls of caps, smoke pours from barrel, perfectly safe, will give endless pleasure and amusement.

Price **10/6**

ASTRA GARAGES

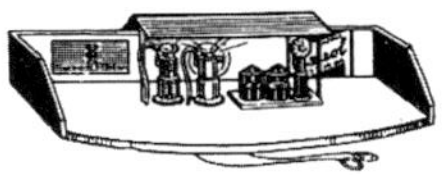

PETROL FILLING STATION, size 12½ in. × 4½ in. finished in colours, complete with Oil Bins, Compressed Air Plant and Petrol Pumps that light up.

Price **3/11**

GARAGE FOR MINIATURE MOTOR CARS, size 12 in. × 10 in., finished in attractive colours, complete with Oil Bins, Air Plant and Petrol Pumps that light up.

Price **5/6**

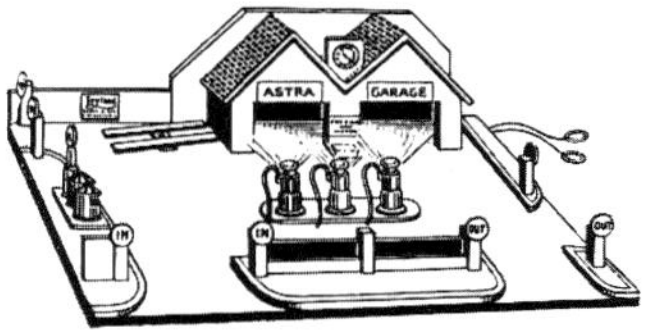

LARGE-SIZE GARAGE, 19 in. × 14 in. complete with Battery and Switch, Oil Bins and Air Plant, and three illuminated Petrol Pumps.

Price **12/6**

59

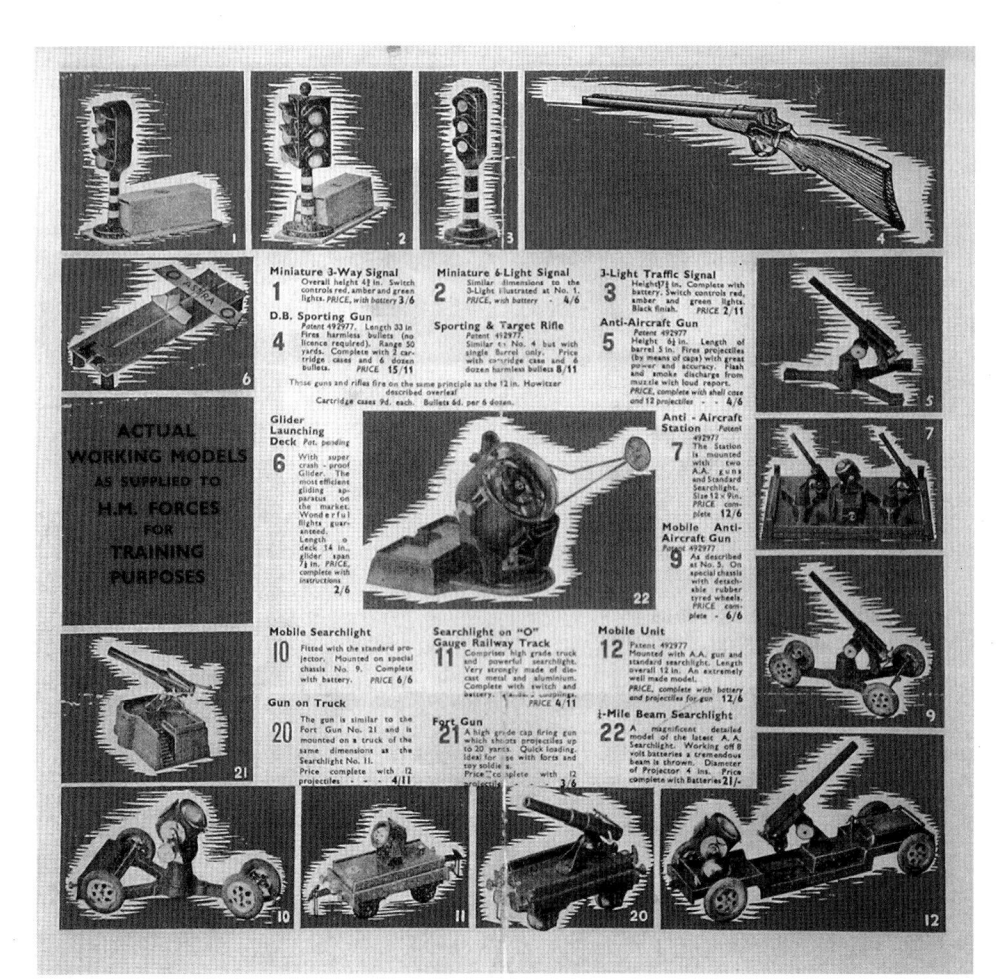

1939 Catalogue

ACTUAL WORKING MODELS AS SUPPLIED TO H.M. FORCES FOR TRAINING PURPOSES

1 Miniature 3-Way Signal
Overall height 4¼ in. Switch controls red, amber and green lights. PRICE, with battery 3/6

2 Miniature 6-Light Signal
Similar dimensions to the 3-Light illustrated at No. 1. PRICE, with battery - 4/6

3 3-Light Traffic Signal
Height 7½ in. Complete with battery. Switch controls red, amber and green lights. Black finish. PRICE 2/11

D.B. Sporting Gun

4 Patent 492977. Length 33 in. Fires harmless bullets (no licence required). Range 50 yards. Complete with 2 cartridge cases and 6 dozen bullets. PRICE 15/11

Sporting & Target Rifle
Patent 492977. Similar to No. 4 but with single barrel only. Price with cartridge case and 6 dozen harmless bullets 8/11

These guns and rifles fire on the same principle as the 12 in. Howitzer described overleaf
Cartridge cases 9d. each. Bullets 6d. per 6 dozen.

5 Anti-Aircraft Gun
Patent 492977
Height 6½ in. Length of barrel 5 in. Fires projectiles (by means of caps) with great power and accuracy. Flash and smoke discharge from muzzle with loud report. PRICE, complete with shell case and 12 projectiles - 4/6

6 Glider Launching Deck Pat. pending
With super crash-proof Glider. The most efficient gliding apparatus on the market. Wonderful flights guaranteed. Length of deck 14 in., glider span 7½ in. PRICE, complete with instructions 2/6

7 Anti-Aircraft Station Patent 492977
The Station is mounted with two A.A. guns and standard Searchlight. Size 12 x 9in. PRICE complete - 12/6

9 Mobile Anti-Aircraft Gun
Patent 492977
As described as No. 5. On special chassis with detachable rubber tyred wheels. PRICE complete - 6/6

10 Mobile Searchlight
Fitted with the standard projector. Mounted on special chassis No. 9. Complete with battery. PRICE 6/6

11 Searchlight on "O" Gauge Railway Track
Comprises high grade truck and powerful searchlight. Very strongly made of diecast metal and aluminium. Complete with switch and battery. PRICE 4/11

12 Mobile Unit
Patent 492977
Mounted with A.A. gun and standard searchlight. Length overall 12 in. An extremely well made model.
PRICE, complete with battery and projectiles for gun 12/6

20 Gun on Truck
The gun is similar to the Fort Gun No. 21 and is mounted on a truck of the same dimensions as the Searchlight No. 11. Price complete with 12 projectiles - 4/11

21 Fort Gun
A high grade cap firing gun which shoots projectiles up to 20 yards. Quick loading. Ideal for use with forts and toy soldiers. Price complete with 12 projectiles 3/6

22 ½-Mile Beam Searchlight
A magnificent detailed model of the latest A.A. Searchlight. Working off 8 volt batteries a tremendous beam is thrown. Diameter of Projector 4 ins. Price complete with Batteries 21/-

1939 Catalogue

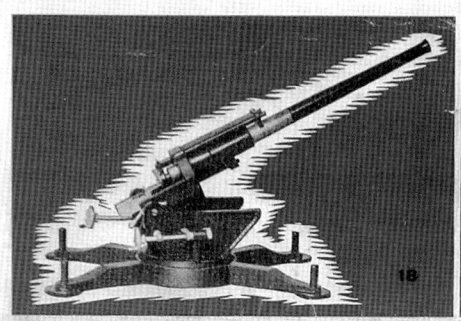

1939 PRICE LIST
All previous Lists cancelled

Super Searchlight
13 Height 8 in. Diameter of Projector 4 in. Elevation and switch operated by control wheels. Throws a powerful beam for great distances. PRICE 8/11

Standard Searchlight
14 Throws a beam of over 100 yards. Height 3½ in. Complete with battery. PRICE 3/6

Morse Signalling Set. Fitted to above. Price complete 4/6 or pair 9/-

Round Base Searchlight
15 A more detailed model of the Standard Searchlight and fitted with larger battery. Throws a beam of 150 yards. Complete with elevating gear. PRICE 4/11

Miniature Searchlight
16 Height 2½ in. Projector swivels and elevates. Gives very powerful beam of light. Fitted with leads and clips for attaching to flash lamp battery. PRICE, less battery - 1/11

12 in. Heavy Howitzer
17 Patent 492977 Range 150 ft. Length, 10½ in. Fitted with elevating mechanism and telescope sighting. Fires harmless rubber projectiles by means of ordinary caps loaded in a shell case as in a real gun. Smoke and flash shoot from muzzle with loud report. Complete with shell case and 6 projectiles. PRICE 10/6 Spare projectiles, 6d. per doz. Spare Shell Cases, 1/- each

3·7 A.A. Gun
18 Patent 492977 This working model of the famous 3·7 Gun is the finest example of its type on the market. With a 9 inch Barrel, automatic Range finding dial, gear operated traverse and elevation controls and breech mechanism; all the features of a real gun are incorporated. Projectiles are fired by means of caps loaded in a shell case as with our other Guns. PRICE complete with 6 dozen projectiles - - 37/6 Spare shell cases 9d. Projectiles 1/- per gross.

ASTRA
BRITISH MADE TOYS OF QUALITY

Sole Manufacturers and Patentees
ASTRA PHAROS
LIMITED
Landor Works, Askew Road
SHEPHERDS BUSH :: W.12
SHEpherds Bush 2472

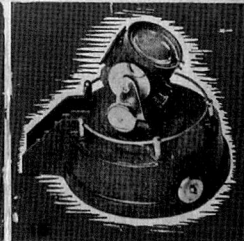

1940 Catalogue

BRITISH MADE — ASTRA — TOYS OF QUALITY

ACTUAL WORKING MODELS AS SUPPLIED TO H.M. FORCES FOR TRAINING PURPOSES

23 Light Anti-Aircraft Gun
An inexpensive but very efficient cap-firing gun; fires with remarkable power and accuracy, giving loud report. Height 4½ ins.
PRICE, complete with projectiles - - - 2/11

PROJECTILES
For all guns, except No. 17 Howitzer.
PRICE 1/- per packet (100)
For No. 17 Howitzer, 6d. per doz.

CAPS
These are not included with the Guns. Any good quality caps can be used, but Astra Special British Made amorces are recommended. PRICE 1/- per doz. boxes (100 Caps in each box)
Postage and Packing, 3d.

5 Anti-Aircraft Gun
Patent 492977
Height 6½ in. Length of barrel 5 in. Fires projectiles (by means of caps) with great power and accuracy. Flash and smoke discharge from muzzle with loud report.
PRICE, complete with shell case and projectiles - 5/6
Spare shell cases 9d. each.

22 ¼-Mile Beam Searchlight
A magnificent detailed model of the latest A.A. Searchlight. Working off 8 volt batteries a tremendous beam is thrown. Diameter of Projector, 4 ins. PRICE complete with Batteries 22/6

7 Anti-Aircraft Station
Patent 492977
The Station is mounted with two A.A. guns and Standard Searchlight. Size 12 × 9in.
PRICE complete - 14/6

21 Fort Gun
A high grade cap firing gun which shoots projectiles up to 20 yards. Quick loading. Ideal for use with forts and toy soldiers. Height 2½ ins.
PRICE, complete with projectiles - - - 3/11

24 Anti-Tank Gun
A fine working model of the latest Mobile Anti-Tank Gun, mounted on chassis with twin Rubber Tyred Wheels. Fires projectiles up to 30 yards range by means of caps. Length overall, 7 ins.
PRICE, complete with projectiles - - - 7/11

9 Mobile Anti-Aircraft Gun
Patent 492977
As described at No. 5. On special chassis with detachable rubber tyred wheels.
PRICE complete with projectiles - - - 7/6

10 Mobile Searchlight
Fitted with the standard projector. Mounted on special chassis with detachable rubber tyred wheels. Complete with battery. PRICE 7/6

12 Mobile Unit
Patent 492977
Mounted with A.A. gun and standard searchlight. Length overall 12 in. An extremely well made model.
PRICE, complete with battery and projectiles for gun 14/6

NOTE. While every effort will be made to prevent any increase in prices, we regret that owing to present conditions we must reserve the right to alter prices and specifications without notice.

1940 Catalogue

Sole Manufacturers, Patentees and Distributors:

ASTRA PHAROS LTD.
LANDOR WORKS, ASKEW ROAD
SHEPHERDS BUSH, LONDON, W.12
Telephone—SHepherds Bush 2472

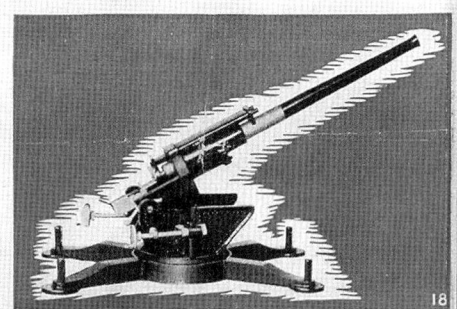

Also obtainable from

18 Super Searchlight
Height 8 in. Diameter of Projector 4 in. Elevation and switch operated by control wheels. Throws a powerful beam for great distances.
PRICE complete with battery 11/6

14 Standard Searchlight
Throws a concentrated beam of light. Height 3½ in. Complete with battery. PRICE 4/6
Adapted for use as Morse Signalling Set.
PRICE complete 5/6

15 Round Base Searchlight
A more detailed model of the Standard Searchlight and fitted with larger battery. Throws a penetrating beam. Complete with elevating gear. Height 3½ ins. PRICE 6/6

16 Miniature Searchlight
Height 2½ in. Projector swivels and elevates. Gives very powerful beam of light. Fitted with leads and clips for attaching to flash lamp battery.
PRICE, less battery 2/6

17 12 in. Heavy Howitzer
Patent 492977
Range 150 ft. Length, 10½ in. Fitted with elevating mechanism and telescope sighting. Fires harmless rubber projectiles by means of ordinary caps loaded in a shell case as in a real gun. Smoke and flash shoot from muzzle with loud report. Complete with shell case and 6 projectiles PRICE 12/6
Spare Projectiles, 6d. per doz.
Spare Shell Cases, 1/- each

18 3.7 A.A. Gun
Patent 492977
This working model of the famous 3.7 gun is the finest example of its type on the market. With a 9-inch barrel, automatic range finding dial, operated traverse and elevation controls and breech mechanism, all the features of a real gun are incorporated. Projectiles are fired by means of caps loaded in a shell case.
PRICE complete with projectiles 42/-
Spare shell cases, 9d. each

ASTRA
BRITISH MADE
TOYS OF QUALITY

1940 PRICE LIST
ALL PREVIOUS LISTS CANCELLED

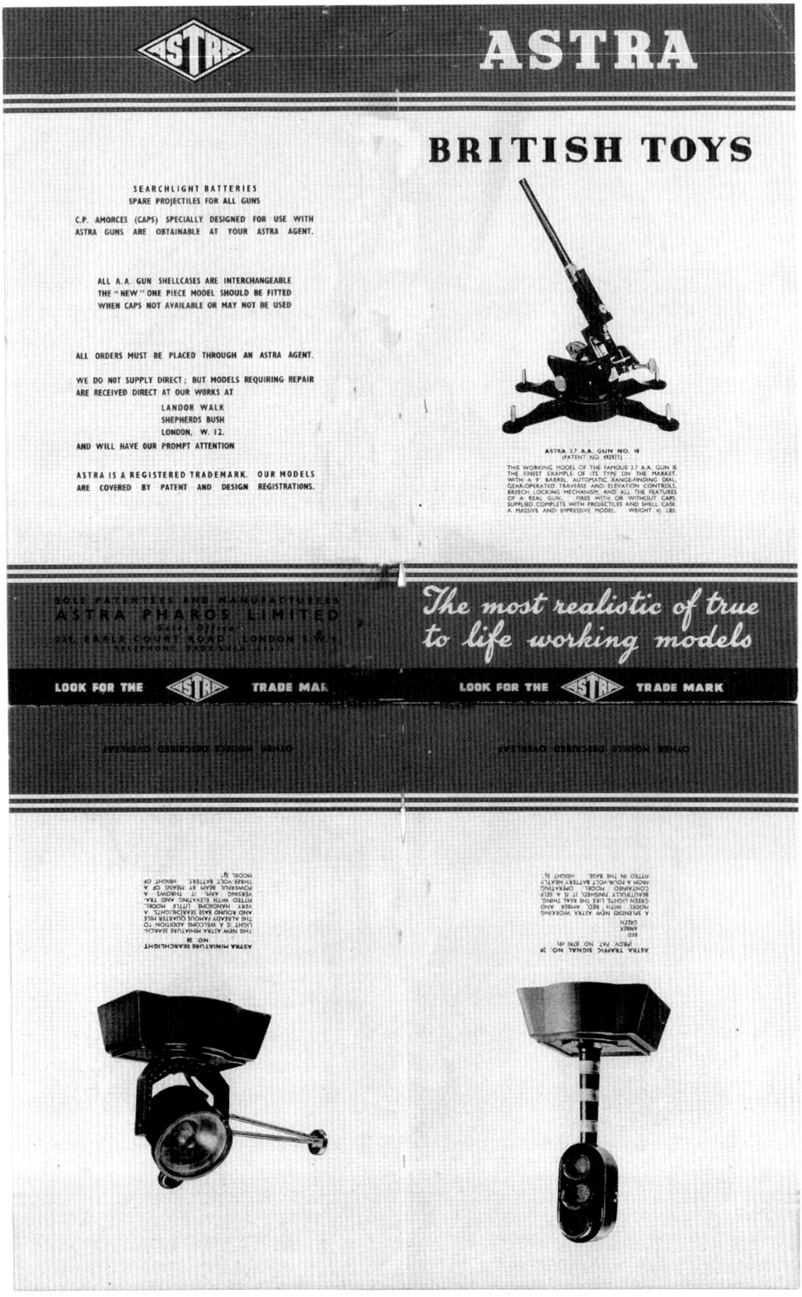

1949 Catalogue

ASTRA

BRITISH TOYS

SEARCHLIGHT BATTERIES
SPARE PROJECTILES FOR ALL GUNS
C.P. AMORCES (CAPS) SPECIALLY DESIGNED FOR USE WITH ASTRA GUNS ARE OBTAINABLE AT YOUR ASTRA AGENT.

ALL A.A. GUN SHELLCASES ARE INTERCHANGEABLE THE "NEW" ONE PIECE MODEL SHOULD BE FITTED WHEN CAPS NOT AVAILABLE OR MAY NOT BE USED

ALL ORDERS MUST BE PLACED THROUGH AN ASTRA AGENT.
WE DO NOT SUPPLY DIRECT; BUT MODELS REQUIRING REPAIR ARE RECEIVED DIRECT AT OUR WORKS AT
LANDOR WALK
SHEPHERDS BUSH
LONDON, W. 12.
AND WILL HAVE OUR PROMPT ATTENTION

ASTRA IS A REGISTERED TRADEMARK. OUR MODELS ARE COVERED BY PATENT AND DESIGN REGISTRATIONS.

ASTRA 3.7 A.A. GUN NO. 19
(PATENT NO. 492827)
THIS WORKING MODEL OF THE FAMOUS 3.7 A.A. GUN IS THE FINEST EXAMPLE OF ITS TYPE ON THE MARKET. WITH A 9" BARREL, AUTOMATIC RANGE-FINDING DIAL, GEAR-OPERATED TRAVERSE AND ELEVATION CONTROLS, BREECH LOCKING MECHANISM, AND ALL THE FEATURES OF A REAL GUN, FIRES WITH OR WITHOUT CAPS. SUPPLIED COMPLETE WITH PROJECTILES AND SHELL CASE. A MASSIVE AND IMPRESSIVE MODEL. WEIGHT 4½ LBS.

SOLE PATENTEES AND MANUFACTURERS
ASTRA PHAROS LIMITED
339, EARLS COURT ROAD, LONDON S.W.5
TELEPHONE: FROBISHER 1655

The most realistic of true to life working models

LOOK FOR THE ASTRA TRADE MARK   LOOK FOR THE ASTRA TRADE MARK

OTHER MODELS DESCRIBED OVERLEAF

ASTRA MINIATURE SEARCHLIGHT NO. 38
THE NEW ASTRA MINIATURE SEARCHLIGHT. IT IS A MARVELOUS ADDITION TO THE ALREADY FAMOUS QUARTER MILE LIGHT (THE MAIN UNIT). A POWERFUL BEAM BY MEANS OF A VERY HANDSOME LITTLE MODEL FITTED WITH ELEVATING AND TRAVERSING MOVEMENTS. LIKE THE REAL THING, A MODEL SAVED AS SEARCHLIGHTS. CONTAINED IN A 4½ VOLT THREE-VOLT BATTERY. WEIGHT OF MODEL, 1½.

ASTRA TRAFFIC SIGNAL NO. 39
(PROV. PAT. NO. 8791/49)
A SPLENDID NEW ASTRA WORKING MODEL MARKED RED, AMBER AND GREEN. BEAUTIFULLY FINISHED. IT IS A SELF CONTAINED MODEL OPERATING FROM A FOUR-VOLT BATTERY NEATLY FITTED IN THE BASE. WEIGHT 1½.

1949 Catalogue

1950 Catalogue

ASTRA — RELIABLE · ROBUST · REALISTIC

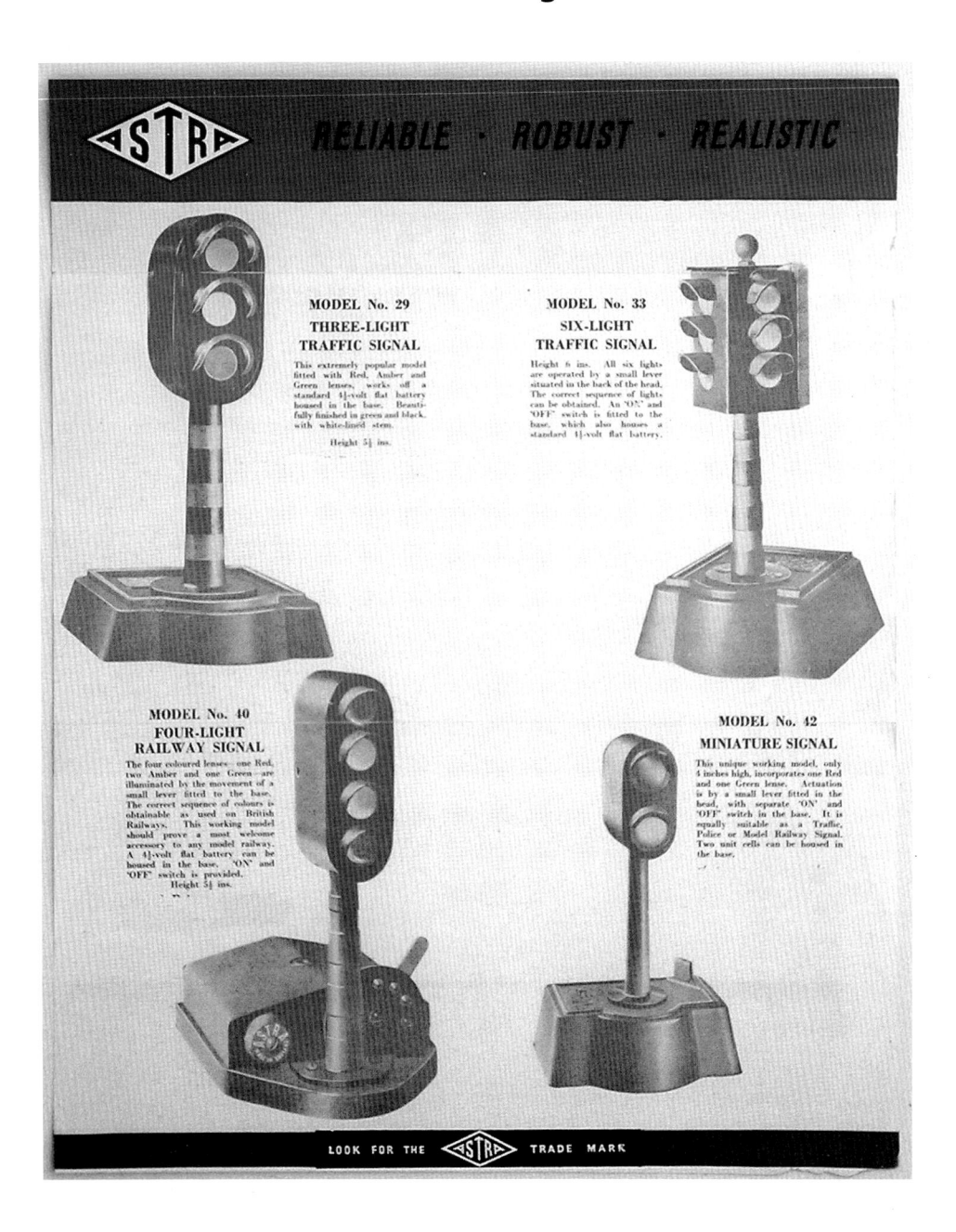

MODEL No. 29
THREE-LIGHT TRAFFIC SIGNAL

This extremely popular model fitted with Red, Amber and Green lenses, works off a standard 4½-volt flat battery housed in the base. Beautifully finished in green and black, with white-lined stem.

Height 5¼ ins.

MODEL No. 33
SIX-LIGHT TRAFFIC SIGNAL

Height 6 ins. All six lights are operated by a small lever situated in the back of the head. The correct sequence of lights can be obtained. An 'ON' and 'OFF' switch is fitted to the base, which also houses a standard 4½-volt flat battery.

MODEL No. 40
FOUR-LIGHT RAILWAY SIGNAL

The four coloured lenses — one Red, two Amber and one Green — are illuminated by the movement of a small lever fitted to the base. The correct sequence of colours is obtainable as used on British Railways. This working model should prove a most welcome accessory to any model railway. A 4½-volt flat battery can be housed in the base. 'ON' and 'OFF' switch is provided.

Height 5¼ ins.

MODEL No. 42
MINIATURE SIGNAL

This unique working model, only 4 inches high, incorporates one Red and one Green lense. Actuation is by a small lever fitted in the head, with separate 'ON' and 'OFF' switch in the base. It is equally suitable as a Traffic, Police or Model Railway Signal. Two unit cells can be housed in the base.

LOOK FOR THE ASTRA TRADE MARK

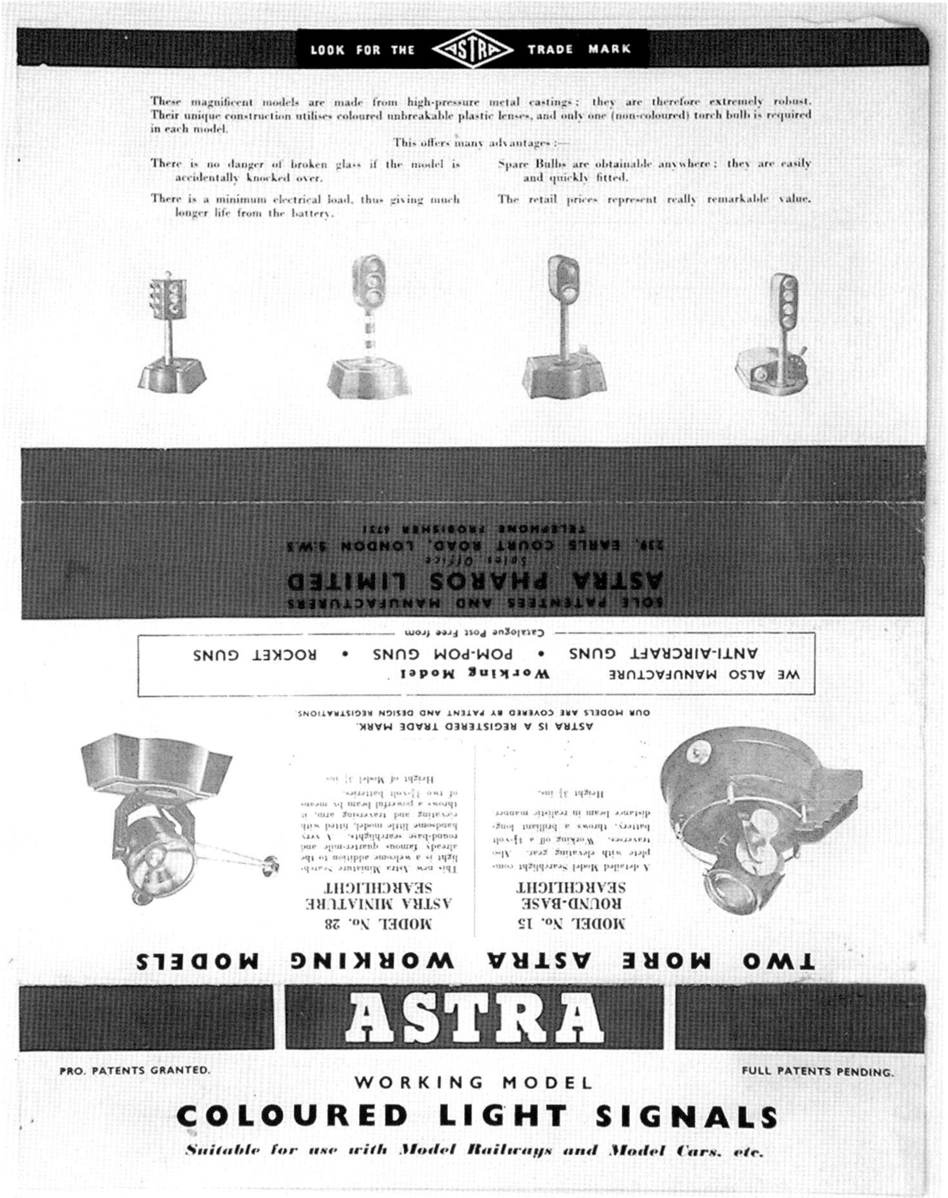

1950 Catalogue

LOOK FOR THE ASTRA TRADE MARK

These magnificent models are made from high-pressure metal castings; they are therefore extremely robust. Their unique construction utilises coloured unbreakable plastic lenses, and only one (non-coloured) torch bulb is required in each model.

This offers many advantages :—

There is no danger of broken glass if the model is accidentally knocked over.

There is a minimum electrical load, thus giving much longer life from the battery.

Spare Bulbs are obtainable anywhere; they are easily and quickly fitted.

The retail prices represent really remarkable value.

TWO MORE ASTRA WORKING MODELS

MODEL No. 15
ROUND-BASE SEARCHLIGHT

A detailed Model Searchlight complete with elevating gear. Also traverses. Working off a 4½-volt battery, throws a brilliant long-distance beam in realistic manner.

Height 3½ ins.

MODEL No. 28
ASTRA MINIATURE SEARCHLIGHT

This new Astra Miniature Searchlight is a welcome addition to the already famous quarter-size and round-base searchlights. A very revealing little model, fitted with handsome universal swivel, it throws a powerful beam to reveal of two 4½-volt batteries.

Height of Model 2½ ins.

ASTRA IS A REGISTERED TRADE MARK. OUR MODELS ARE COVERED BY PATENT AND DESIGN REGISTRATIONS.

WE ALSO MANUFACTURE **Working Model** ANTI-AIRCRAFT GUNS • POM-POM GUNS • ROCKET GUNS

Catalogue Post Free from

ASTRA PHAROS LIMITED
Sales Office
239, EARLS COURT ROAD, LONDON S.W.5
TELEPHONE FROBISHER 1731

SOLE PATENTEES AND MANUFACTURERS

ASTRA

PRO. PATENTS GRANTED.   FULL PATENTS PENDING.

WORKING MODEL
COLOURED LIGHT SIGNALS
Suitable for use with Model Railways and Model Cars, etc.

Instruction Leaflets

Instruction leaflets for the models produced prior to the Military Range were quite detailed and printed on good quality white paper. Inexplicably this paper was gummed on the back and so the survival rate is rather low. The illustration of the instructions for the Floodlighting Set date from 1936.

By 1937 the paper had lost its gummed back but was still white and of good quality. The illustrated instructions for the Heavy Howitzer priced at 10/6d are a good example. From early 1939 instruction leaflets were printed on much cheaper buff coloured paper. The illustrations of the instructions for the 3.7 AA Gun and later Heavy Howitzer are from this period.

From 1940 until the end of toy production, leaflets became very simple affairs with only brief instructions. They were printed on thin cheap paper in a variety of pale colours.

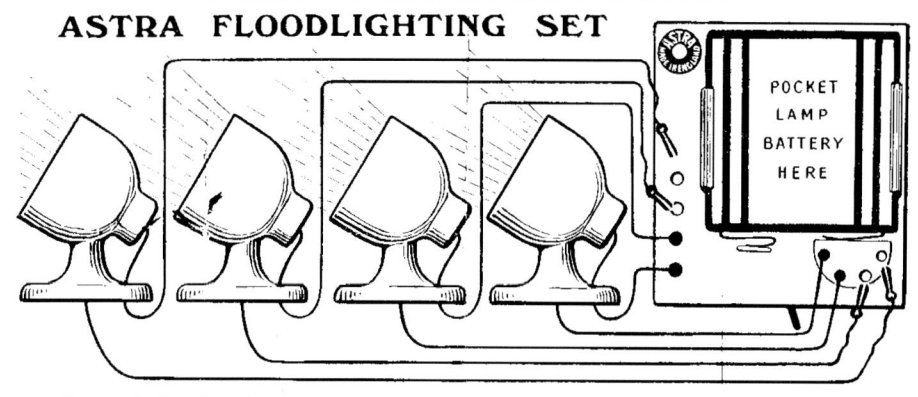

DIAGRAM OF CONNECTIONS FOR WIRING
ASTRA FLOODLIGHTING SET

POCKET LAMP BATTERY HERE

Pins are fitted to the ends of the wires from the floodlights.

To connect correctly place one pin from each floodlight into one of the holes at the side of the switch plate, then place the remaining pin from each floodlight into a hole in the semi circular contact plate.

By movement of the switch lever, the floodlights can be switched 'on' or 'off' at will.

INSTRUCTIONS FOR ASTRA 3·7 A.A. GUN (Patent No 492977)

Read these Instructions before attempting to handle the Gun

TRAVERSE AND ELEVATION

ON NO ACCOUNT SHOULD ANY ATTEMPT BE MADE TO MOVE THE BARREL BY HAND. THE OPERATING WHEELS ONLY MUST BE USED BOTH TO ELEVATE AND TRAVERSE THE GUN.

The elevation control is operated by means of the wheel on the right-hand side of the breech, which should be turned in an ANTI-CLOCKWISE DIRECTION to elevate, and in a CLOCKWISE direction to depress.

ON NO ACCOUNT MUST THIS WHEEL BE FORCED to depress the barrel after this has attained a horizontal position and is resting against the mechanism underneath, otherwise damage will be done to the gears.

To traverse the gun, an operating wheel is mounted on the left-hand side of the Base. The small grub screw on the side of the base below the range finding dial is provided to take up any play which may develop in the traversing gear after long service.

THE RANGE FINDING DIAL on the right hand side of the gun shows elevation from 0 to 90 degrees. DO NOT ATTEMPT to move the pointer by hand. This is geared to the mechanism and works automatically.

TO LOAD THE GUN

Pull back the hammer by means of the finger and thumb until it engages with the trigger catch and is held back. Move the breech locking lever situated at the back of the breech, over to the LEFT which will free the locking device behind the Shell Case and enable this to be withdrawn. Unscrew the back of the Shell Case and place from one to three ordinary paper caps in the recess thus exposed, AND SCREW ON THE BACK OF THE SHELL CASE AGAIN. (One cap is enough for short range, and three gives maximum range.) The projectile is then placed in the recess in the front of the Shell Case, and the Shell pushed back into the breech. The locking lever must now be turned to the RIGHT so that the cam rises and holds the Shell Case firmly into the breech of the gun. Blank shots fired without a projectile produce a loud report with realistic flash and smoke emitted from the muzzle.

TO FIRE THE GUN

PRESS DOWN the Nickle Plated trigger release situated on the left-hand side behind the hammer.

IMPORTANT

It is essential that all the gears and moving parts ARE OILED OCCASIONALLY WITH THIN OIL. Use grease for the gears. The Shell Case must be KEPT FREE from used caps, and the SMALL HOLE IN THE CAP RECESS KEPT CLEAR. The striking plunger should MOVE FREELY through the back of the Shell Case and the application of a little paraffin or thin oil will prevent any tendency to stick. The breech chamber into which the Shell Case fits must also be kept clean otherwise the Shell Case will not fit correctly into position.

Spare Shell Cases can be supplied at 9d. each; spare projectiles at 6d. per 6 dozen.

Provided the above instructions are carried out, and good quality caps used, the gun will give complete satisfaction. Should difficulty be experienced in obtaining good caps, we can supply a first-class make, at 1s. per 12 boxes (100 caps in each box).

ASTRA · PHAROS LIMITED
LANDOR WORKS, ASKEW ROAD, LONDON, W. 12 (Telephone: SHEpherds Bush 2472)

12" HEAVY HOWITZER

PRICE **10/6**

RANGE **50** YARDS

Complete with shell case and 6 Projectiles

Length Overall 6¼ in.

REG. DES. 835157

Simple to operate. Cannot go wrong. Beautifully made. Fires harmless rubber projectiles by means of ordinary caps, up to 50 yards range.

Fitted with correct elevating mechanism and telescope sighting. Breech loading. Smoke and flash discharged entirely from the muzzle.

Nothing has ever been made to approach this true working model for simplicity, power and amazing value. Pneumatic pressure created inside the shell case by a patented design, with ordinary caps, produces this exceptional efficiency.

The firing is so accurate and powerful that proper shooting competitions and games can be enjoyed with ordinary caps—obtainable at any toy shop—loading takes only a few seconds.

INSTRUCTIONS

TO LOAD. Pull back hammer until trigger engages. Pull shell case out of breech. Unscrew back of shell case. Place from 1 to 4 caps, according to the range required, in the cup thus exposed in the front part of the shell case. Screw on back of shell case firmly. Fit rubber projectile gently into front opening of shell case. Push shell into breech of gun as far as it will go. The gun is now ready to fire. Push shots fired without a projectile produce a loud report with realistic discharge of smoke and flash from the muzzle.

TO FIRE. Pull firing lever on right side of breech.

ELEVATING GEAR. Turn wheel clockwise to depress—anti-clockwise to elevate. Do not force beyond normal limits. For quick action press down the elevating wheel, thereby disengaging the gear drive. The gun can then be elevated or depressed by hand without using the elevating gear or disengaging the drive. The divisions indicated by the elevator pointer correspond to 10 yards increase or decrease in range.

CARE OF WORKING PARTS. Keep breech, shell case, hole in cup container, and plunger free from exploded caps. The plunger must move freely. Oil all working parts occasionally with thin oil.

NOTE. Never attempt to fire the gun without screwing on the back of the shell case properly—leakage, with loss of power, will result, and the back may blow off.

SPARE SHELL CASES   ..   ..   1/- each
SPARE RUBBER PROJECTILES   ..   ..   6d. per dozen

ASTRA PHAROS LTD.

Sole Manufacturers, Patentees and Distributors:—

LANDOR ROAD WORKS, SHEPHERDS BUSH, LONDON, W.12

Phone : SHEpherds Bush 2472

12" HEAVY HOWITZER

RANGE **50** YARDS

PATENT No. 482977

Supplied Complete with shell case and 6 Projectiles. Length Overall 10¼ in.

Simple to operate. Cannot go wrong. Beautifully made. Fires harmless rubber projectiles by means of ordinary caps, up to 50 yards range. Fitted with correct elevating mechanism and telescope sighting. Breech loading. Smoke and flash discharged entirely from the muzzle.

Nothing has ever been made to approach this true working model for simplicity, power and amazing value. Pneumatic pressure created inside the shell case by a patented design, with ordinary caps, produces this exceptional efficiency.

The firing is so accurate and powerful that proper shooting competitions and games can be enjoyed with ordinary caps—obtainable at any toy shop—loading takes only a few seconds.

INSTRUCTIONS

TO LOAD. Pull back hammer until trigger engages. Pull shell case out of breech. Unscrew back of shell case. Place from 1 to 4 caps, according to the range required, in the cup thus exposed in the front part of the shell case. Screw on back of shell case firmly. Fit rubber projectile gently into front opening of shell case. Push shell into breech of gun as far as it will go. The gun is now ready to fire. Blank shots fired without a projectile produce a loud report with realistic discharge of smoke and flash from the muzzle.

TO FIRE. Lift firing lever on right side of breech.

ELEVATING GEAR. Turn wheel clockwise to depress—anti-clockwise to elevate. Do not force beyond normal limits. For quick action press down the elevating wheel, thereby disengaging the gear drive. The gun can then be elevated or depressed by hand.

NEVER TRY to force barrel up or down without using the elevating gear or disengaging the drive. The divisions indicated by the elevator pointer correspond to 10 yards increase or decrease in range.

CARE OF WORKING PARTS. Keep breech, shell case, hole in cup container, and plunger free from exploded caps. The plunger must move freely. Oil all working parts occasionally with thin oil.

NOTE. Never attempt to fire the gun without screwing on the back of the shell case properly—leakage, with loss of power, will result, and the back may blow off.

SPARE SHELL CASES   ..   ..   1/- each
SPARE RUBBER PROJECTILES   ..   ..   6d. per dozen

ASTRA PHAROS LTD.

Sole Manufacturers, Patentees and Distributors

LANDOR WORKS, SHEPHERDS BUSH, LONDON, W.12

Telephone : SHEpherds Bush 2472

INSTRUCTIONS

TO LOAD.—Pull back hammer until trigger engages. Place an ordinary paper cap in the recess thus exposed. Slide a projectile down the muzzle

TO FIRE.—Depress firing lever.

CARE OF WORKING PARTS.— Oil hammer mechanism occasionally. Keep the cap recess free from cap paper, and the small hole in the centre clear.

SOLE MANUFACTURERS:
ASTRA-PHAROS, LTD., LANDOR WORKS, SHEPHERDS BUSH, LONDON, W.12.
Telephone: SHEpherds Bush 2472

INSTRUCTIONS

TO LOAD.—Pull back hammer until trigger engages. Place an ordinary paper cap in the recess thus exposed. Slide a projectile down the muzzle.

TO FIRE.—Depress firing lever.

CARE OF WORKING PARTS.— Oil hammer mechanism occasionally. Keep the cap recess free from cap paper, and the small hole in the centre clear.

SOLE MANUFACTURERS:
ASTRA-PHAROS, LTD., LANDOR WORKS, SHEPHERDS BUSH, LONDON, W.12.
Telephone: SHEpherds Bush 2472

INSTRUCTIONS FOR CARE AND OPERATION OF ASTRA GUN ON TRUCK AND FORT GUN

TO LOAD.—Pull back hammer until trigger engages. Place an ordinary paper cap in the recess thus exposed. Slide a projectile down the muzzle.

TO FIRE.—Depress firing lever.

CARE OF WORKING PARTS.— Oil hammer mechanism occasionally. Keep the cap recess free from cap paper, and the small hole in the centre clear.

SOLE MANUFACTURERS:
ASTRA - PHAROS, LTD., LANDOR WORKS, SHEPHERDS BUSH, LONDON, W.12.
Telephone: SHEpherds Bush 2472

PATENT 492877

BY USING THE SPECIAL SINGLE PIECE SHELL CASE OUR Nos. 5, 18 & 26, A.A. GUNS WILL SHOOT WITHOUT USING CAPS (AMORCES)

To load the gun pull back the hammer until trigger engages; remove shell case from breech. Place a shouldered pellet in the single piece shell case, allowing the small end of the pellet to project through the back of the case.

Push shell case home in the breech.

The shell case with the screw on back should be used when caps are utilised to eject the pellet; see separate instruction sheet.

ASTRA-PHAROS, LTD., LANDOR WORKS, ASKEW ROAD, LONDON, W.12.
Telephone: SHEpherds Bush 2472

INSTRUCTIONS FOR CONNECTING AND FITTING BATTERY
— FLAT BATTERY —

Remove battery sealing strip and slide ring clip on end of wire on to long battery contact—if necessary double back long contact on to top of battery to keep it clear of short contact. Press battery into battery clip, with short contact adjacent to switch screw.

ASTRA-PHAROS, LTD., LANDOR WORKS, ASKEW ROAD, LONDON, W.12.
Telephone: SHEpherds Bush 2472

Astra- Pharos Letterhead

MANUFACTURING ELECTRICAL AND MECHANICAL ENGINEERS

ASTRA

Patentees of
ASTRA
TOYS AND MODELS

ASTRA PHAROS LIMITED
LANDOR WORKS
ASKEW ROAD,
LONDON, W.12

Directors:
F. Y. U. Weldon. A.M.Inst.B.E.
D. M. Stow

Telephones:
SHEpherds Bush 2472
4607

Oct 17th 1955

Your Ref.   Our Ref.

<u>To whom it may concern</u>

This is to certify that Mr. W. Hewitt has been in our employ for over twenty years. During this time we have found him to be honest, trustworthy and a very capable foreman; he is also a skilled lathe operator and tool maker. He left at his own request to obtain more renumerative employment.

for ASTRA PHAROS Ltd

F Y Weldon
Director.